The Dysfunctional Congress?

Dilemmas in American Politics

Series Editor   **L. Sandy Maisel,** *Colby College*

Dilemmas in American Politics offers teachers and students a series of quality books on timely topics and key institutions in American government. Each text will examine a "real world" dilemma and will be structured to cover the historical, theoretical, policy relevant, and future dimensions of its subject.

••

BOOKS IN THIS SERIES

The Dysfunctional Congress?

The Individual Roots of an Institutional Dilemma

Kenneth R. Mayer
University of Wisconsin–Madison

David T. Canon
University of Wisconsin–Madison

Westview Press
A Member of the Perseus Books Group

To our children:
Adam and Sydney
and
Neal, Katherine, and Sophia

Dilemmas in American Politics

Copyright © 1999 by Westview Press, A Member of the Perseus Books Group

Published in 1999 in the United States of America by Westview Press, 5500 Central Avenue, Boulder, Colorado 80301-2877, and in the United Kingdom by Westview Press, 12 Hid's Copse Road, Cumnor Hill, Oxford OX2 9JJ

Library of Congress Cataloging-in-Publication Data
Mayer, Kenneth R., 1960–
   The dysfunctional Congress? : the individual roots of an
institutional dilemma / Kenneth R. Mayer and David T. Canon [sic].
      p.   cm. — (Dilemmas in American politics)
   Includes bibliographical references and index.
   ISBN 0-8133-2698-2 (hc). — ISBN 0-8133-2699-0 (pbk.)
   1. United States. Congress.   2. United States. Congress—Reform.
I. Canon, David T.   II. Title.   III. Series.
JK1041.M39   1999
328.73'0704—dc21   98-55277
                                                                        CIP

The paper used in this publication meets the requirements of the American National Standard for Permanence of Paper for Printed Library Materials Z39.48-1984.

10   9   8   7   6   5   4   3   2   1

The Dysfunctional Congress?

The Individual Roots of an Institutional Dilemma

Kenneth R. Mayer
University of Wisconsin–Madison

David T. Canon
University of Wisconsin–Madison

Westview Press
A Member of the Perseus Books Group

To our children:
Adam and Sydney
and
Neal, Katherine, and Sophia

Dilemmas in American Politics

Published in 1999 in the United States of America by Westview Press, 5500 Central Avenue, Boulder, Colorado 80301-2877, and in the United Kingdom by Westview Press, 12 Hid's Copse Road, Cumnor Hill, Oxford OX2 9JJ

Library of Congress Cataloging-in-Publication Data
Mayer, Kenneth R., 1960–
    The dysfunctional Congress? : the individual roots of an
institutional dilemma / Kenneth R. Mayer and David T. Canon [sic].
        p.   cm. — (Dilemmas in American politics)
    Includes bibliographical references and index.
    ISBN 0-8133-2698-2 (hc). — ISBN 0-8133-2699-0 (pbk.)
    1. United States. Congress.   2. United States. Congress—Reform.
I. Canon, David T.   II. Title.   III. Series.
JK1041.M39   1999
328.73'0704—dc21   98-55277
                                                                                        CIP

The paper used in this publication meets the requirements of the American National Standard for Permanence of Paper for Printed Library Materials Z39.48-1984.

10   9   8   7   6   5   4   3   2   1

Contents

3 The Collective Dilemma in the Modern Context   65

4 The Collective Dilemma and Congressional Reform   97

5 An Agenda for Reform: Coming to Terms with the Collective Dilemma   133

Tables and Illustrations

Preface

In our undergraduate courses on Congress, which we have taught over the past decade, we often find ourselves in the position of defending Congress against the common charge that it is completely out of touch with the public. Political scientists, it seems, view the legislative process with far more sympathy than most people, even more than representatives and senators, who are quick to berate the institution. Our students often are puzzled by our insistence that Congress is not that bad, when everyone knows that it is corrupt and inept.

What we have attempted to do in this volume is explain why Congress acts as it does, and why so much of that activity undermines the institution, both in terms of how it functions and where it stands in the public eye. In doing so, we introduce students to an argument using "rational choice" theories to explain what happens when individuals come together to make collective decisions. We argue that Congress is fundamentally beset by a collective dilemma, because behavior that is individually rational to legislators results in a collective situation that none of them would otherwise prefer. Members pursuing their own election interests, representing their constituents, and locating themselves within the institution often act in ways that hurt the institution. Far from being a consequence of venal and ambitious legislators, this is a basic consequence of representative democracy. Even the Framers, in all their wisdom, grossly overestimated how devoted the first legislators would be to the collective good instead of local constituency interests.

The emphasis on the collective dilemma concept also provides a framework for thinking about how various reform proposals would affect Congress. In our view, reforms that would centralize control within the institution have the best chance of raising the visibility of collective issues; yet we argue that centralization and efficiency come at a price, and that these goals must be balanced against the competing, and equally valid, values of openness and participation. That is the fundamental question of democratic politics, and it cannot be resolved in any other way than through the political process itself.

In writing this book, we benefited from the support of the Sophomore Summer Honors Research Apprenticeship Program in the College of Letters and Science, University of Wisconsin–Madison, and of the Department of Political Science; through these sources we were able to secure the valuable research assistance of

Jesse Gray and Chris Stangl. Our project editor, Kristin Milavec, did an extraordinary job, as did our copy editor, Sharon DeJohn. Everyone we dealt with at Westview was efficient and professional. We are also indebted to Leo Wiegman, our editor at Westview, and Sandy Maisel, for their vision and patience. We also thank our wives, Susan and Sarah, whose patience we tested more than Leo's and Sandy's.

Kenneth R. Mayer
David T. Canon

Introduction

In the midst of the congressional session, one legislator introduced a bill to raise members' salaries after an effort in the previous Congress had been voted down decisively. Supporters of the pay raise argued that inflation had seriously eroded legislators' earnings, and they noted that the cost of living had doubled over the previous twenty-five years. In an effort to deal with the issue as quietly as possible, the leadership hustled the bill through committee and floor debate in only four days. The bill passed on a narrow vote that no doubt reflected fears that the public would react badly to the notion of a congressional pay raise.

Those fears were well grounded. The negative reaction was immediate and intense: media reports and editorials criticized a doubling of congressional pay, and "public indignation, fanned by the press, was aroused to such heights that according to contemporaries it was without precedent" in American history. The public perceived that Congress was enriching itself while raising taxes on ordinary citizens, all at a time of economic hardship (never mind that this same Congress had cut taxes, and that the economy was in fact growing steadily). At the next congressional election, an infuriated electorate threw out incumbents in extraordinary numbers, and chastened legislators repealed the pay increase in a lame duck session that took place before the new Congress convened.

Close observers of congressional politics might recognize this as the story of the abortive 1989 congressional pay raise, in which popular opposition ultimately forced Congress to back down from its proposal to increase salaries by 51 percent. Yet these events took place not in 1989, but in 1816 and 1817, with the remarkable similarities between the two events highlighting important common themes about public attitudes toward Congress.[1] Thomas Jefferson took note of the events in correspondence with Albert Gallatin in 1817: "I have never known so unanimous a sentiment of disapprobation. . . . I confess I was highly pleased with this proof of the innate good sense, the vigilance, and the determination of the people to act for themselves (letter to Albert Gallatin, June 16, 1817, from Ford 1899, 90). On the question of repealing the increase, North Carolina Representative Lewis

1

Williams wrote his constituents in 1817 using language that could just as well have applied in 1990: "The compensation law, as it is commonly called, or the law in relation to the pay of members of Congress, has been repealed. This subject produced much animated discussion—having opposed the law at its passage, I voted for its repeal in every shape in which the question was presented" (letter, March 1, 1817; Cunningham 1978, I, 1005–1006).

Politics, economics, culture, and technology were all vastly different in 1816 and 1989, but the public reaction to Congress raising its own pay was identical.

Consider the following remarks by a retiring member of Congress after decades of service in the House:

> Forty years ago there was no propaganda; certainly no organized agencies and lobbies. Bills then originated in committees and represented the mature thought of members. Now they are written and forced through Congress by outside organizations . . . [legislators] had an opportunity to study legislation and could vote intelligently. Now the lobbyist comes to you and says 'We want this,' and generally he gets it.

This sounds very much like a complaint that could have been made in 1998, but in fact it is from Joseph Cannon (R–Ill.), speaking in 1923 and recalling wistfully—and inaccurately—the efficient days of the 1880s (MacNeil 1963, 205–206).

Finally, a Brookings Institution/American Enterprise Institute report on legislative reform offered the following summary of prevailing attitudes toward Congress:

> [Today] Congress bashing is a sport enjoyed (or at least engaged in) by one and all. Network news programs and radio talk shows drip with contempt for a Congress whose penchant for scandal and scramble for pork, in the views of producers and anchors, provide ample material and transparent justification for their increasingly negative coverage. Why should news professionals be reticent about bashing Congress, when many of its own members regularly denounce their institution with vitriolic rhetoric ready made for the evening news? (Mann and Ornstein 1993, 2).

Public attitudes toward and criticisms of Congress have shown a remarkable consistency over the years, with the same themes arising again and again. This suggests that opinion about Congress is driven by some constant dynamics, not by the idiosyncrasies of particular pieces of legislation or member failings.

At the same time, many observers point out that Congress seems more and more to be operating in a constant state of crisis and gridlock. Despite pressing national problems—the globalization of trade, breathtaking technological advances, an impending crisis in entitlements—Congress appears powerless to respond.

Rather than deliberate and act on these issues, these critics maintain, legislators content themselves with meaningless symbolic acts and endless partisan bickering, while public approval of the institution sinks lower and lower. The institutional capacity of Congress to deal with these problems has been undermined by recent developments, such as the rise of television, the proliferation of interest groups, the decline of political parties as a mobilizing force in American politics, and the increasing complexity of modern problems. Our contention is that public attitudes toward Congress are in large measure driven by qualities inherent to systems of geographic representation (in which defined geographic regions elect representatives who serve in a national deliberative body), candidate-centered elections, and the collective nature of Congress as an institution, rather than any recent political developments (although the factors outlined above have exacerbated Congress's collective dilemmas). These characteristics of our political system produce two types of collective dilemmas for Congress: an institutional dilemma and a policy dilemma. The former arises when the political and electoral interests of individual legislators conflict with the institutional needs of the legislature. The latter is produced when members respond to their geographic constituencies and promote local interests over the collective good. In both instances, individual legislators face incentives to act in ways that ultimately damage Congress as an institution.

The Institutional Dilemma

The institutional dilemma comes from two types of behavior: (1) open criticism of Congress by members who tear down its reputation in order to secure partisan or personal advantage; and (2) members' unwillingness to pay the costs of institutional maintenance (the types of activities that hold the institution together and keep it from flying apart in 535 different directions).

The phenomenon of legislators and challengers bashing the institution in which they serve was identified by Richard Fenno as "running for Congress by running against Congress." Fenno, one of the keenest observers of Congress, was greatly surprised by the prevalence of this behavior:

> Nothing [had] prepared me to discover that each member of Congress polishes his or her individual reputation at the expense of the institutional reputation of Congress. In explaining what he was doing in Washington, every one of the eighteen House members took the opportunity to picture himself as different from, and better than, most of his fellow members of Congress. None availed himself of the opportunity to educate his constituents about Congress as an institution—not in any way that would "hurt a little." To the contrary, the members' process of differentiating themselves

from the Congress as a whole only served, directly or indirectly, to downgrade the Congress (Fenno 1978, 164).

The advantage of this strategy is that, at least in the short term, it is completely "ubiquitous, addictive, cost-free, and foolproof" (Fenno 1978, 168). Yet in the long term the costs become apparent, in the form of an erosion in public support of the institution. Having heard so many legislators run down the institution for so long, the public cannot help but view Congress in a sinister light. The collective dilemma comes into play. According to Fenno, "In the short run, everybody plays and everybody wins. Yet the institution bleeds from 435 separate cuts. In the long run, therefore, somebody may lose" (Fenno 1978, 168). As we demonstrate in Chapter 3, running against Congress is not a recent development, having been present since Congress's earliest days. Historical evidence supports our claim that the collective dilemma is an inherent characteristic of any representative assembly.

The institutional dilemma also arises when members are not willing to participate in the activities that sustain the long-term health of the institution. David Mayhew, in his classic work *Congress: The Electoral Connection*, stated the problem succinctly:

> If members hope to spend careers in Congress, they have a stake in maintaining its prestige as an institution. They also have a stake in maintaining congressional control over resources that are useful in electoral quests. But if every member pursues only his own electoral goals, the prestige and power of the institution will drain away (Mayhew 1974, 145).

Individual legislators have little incentive to take care of the institution, and find it much more politically profitable to let others perform maintenance tasks while they themselves attend to their own electoral and political interests. The more freedom individual legislators have to act autonomously, and the less institutional patriotism (Uslaner 1993) members have, the more the institution will suffer.

Members are acting rationally when they bash the institution and "free ride," allowing others to do the time-consuming tasks of institutional maintenance. This self-interested behavior helps them get reelected. However, while it is individually rational to behave in this fashion, it produces a collective outcome that is in nobody's interest: a weakened institution that is held in low regard by the public.[2]

The Policy Dilemma

The second type of collective dilemma comes from the inherent tension in any representative assembly between national and local interests. That is, members are responsible for enacting policies for the "general good," which may require them to subordinate local interests to the good of the whole. On the other hand, individual legislators must also represent local attitudes and work to protect and promote the interests of their constituents, which may not be consistent with collective interests. For example, a senator from a state heavily populated with military contractors has an incentive to keep defense spending high even if there is otherwise little need for large defense budgets. A representative from an agricultural district has an incentive to protect farm subsidies and price supports, even if it means more taxes and higher food prices for everyone else. The more "representative" Congress is, the more voice local interests will have in legislation. Undoubtedly, perceptions of what constitutes the "general good" depend heavily on one's values and attitudes toward particular programs, but it is not difficult to come up with similar examples, across a broad range of political perspectives.

We all agree the IRS is out of control. TOLES © 1991 & 1997 the *Buffalo News*. Reprinted with permission of UNIVERSAL PRESS SYNDICATE. All rights reserved.

In posing this policy dilemma we do not assume that district interests are "bad" and collective or national interests are "good." There are many instances in which a member of Congress is performing a proper representative function by defending his or her district's interests, even when those interests may not serve the broader collective good. For example, in the mid-1990s a strong consensus emerged that the welfare system was "broken" and needed to be reformed. A strong bipartisan majority in Congress passed the Personal Responsibility Act in 1996 and President Clinton signed it into law. However, a substantial minority of members in Congress opposed the changes, either on general policy grounds or because they believed the changes would adversely affect a substantial number of their constituents (one hundred House members and twenty-one senators voted against final passage). While one could argue that these members were attempting to undermine the collective will, they were providing an important voice for their districts' or states' interests. Other district interests that may not elicit as much sympathy as children in poverty who are denied benefits under the new welfare law, such as tobacco price supports, are also legitimately protected by members who are fulfilling their representative obligations.

The Framers themselves were torn between their belief that politicians would recognize their obligation to the nation as a whole and a recognition that sectional rivalries were inevitable; ultimately they could not resolve the tension and set out a number of contradictory positions regarding the character of legislatures. In *Federalist* 57, Madison claimed that the first aim of every political constitution is "to obtain for rulers men who possess most wisdom to discern, and most virtue to pursue, the common good of society," even as he defended the method of elected House members as "involving every security which can be devised or desired for their fidelity to their constituents" (350, 351). In *Federalist* 10, Madison acknowledged to the critics of the various state constitutions, "that the public good is disregarded in the conflicts of rival parties, and that measures are too often decided, not according to the rules of justice and the rights of the minor parties, but by the superior force of an interested and overbearing majority" (77), even as he held up the republican view of government as a way to "refine and enlarge the public views by passing them through the medium of a chosen body of citizens, whose wisdom may best discern the true interest of their country and whose patriotism and love of justice will be least likely to sacrifice it to temporary or partial considerations" (82), and spoke of legislators with "enlightened views and virtuous sentiments" (85–86). The Framers were confident that a republican government would be characterized by "civic harmony, selfless behavior, and consensus upon a national public good" (Sharp 1993, 3).

Members have created various institutions and processes—committees, parties, complicated parliamentary procedures—to reduce the likelihood that the policy dilemma will emerge and to enhance the possibility of fulfilling the Founders' ideals. Also, there are many types of legislation that do not pit national against local interests, such as consensual "mom and apple pie issues" that pass by nearly unanimous votes or policies with universal application that do not have any obvious geographic component, such as the new Roth Individual Retirement Accounts, college savings programs, or eliminating the "marriage penalty" in the tax code. But these institutions and consensual or national issues do not—and, we argue, cannot—completely mitigate the policy dilemma.

In fact there are strong individual incentives for members to pursue local interests while neglecting national concerns. Just as members have little incentive to engage in the hard work of institutional maintenance, Mayhew argues that there is little incentive to get down to the difficult task of formulating national legislation, which involves the time-consuming jobs of backroom bargaining and coalition building. Instead, according to Mayhew, members are more likely to engage in "advertising," by which he simply means getting the incumbent's name out before the public in a positive manner by appearing at homecoming parades, addressing high school audiences, or sending out letters of congratulation and the like, and in "credit claiming" for particularized benefits that are delivered to the district or for constituency services performed by the member's office (1974, 49–59). Furthermore, institutionalized practices such as "logrolling," whereby members trade votes for support on each others' local projects or legislation, makes the collective dilemma all the more likely. If the collective dilemma could be rooted out by simply voting down the narrow, geographic interests that all members have, policies such as dairy price supports and tobacco subsidies would have been eliminated long ago. However, if members stick together in supporting each others' pet projects, overcoming the collective dilemma is a much more formidable task.

Implications of the Collective Dilemma

The policy and institutional dilemmas create a situation in which individual legislators find it in their rational self-interest to behave in ways that are detrimental to the collective interest of Congress as an institution, as well as to the collective good of society. Put simply, individual rationality by legislators produces collectively irrational institutional and policy results. This tension between representativeness and efficient lawmaking, between individual and institutional prestige, has several important implications:

1. The collective dilemma is the main reason Congress is held in such low esteem by the American public. As political scientists have long recognized, people tend to dislike Congress (often intensely) even when they think their own representative is doing a good job. This dichotomy is directly linked to a persistent feature in American political culture, the belief that there is an objective national interest that should overwhelm particularistic and local differences.

2. The dilemma creates an imbalance between individual and institutional needs—a "disequilibrium," to use the terminology of rational choice theory: rank-and-file members promote a decentralization of power within the legislature, while at the same time recognizing the need for centralized policymaking capacity; there is a general lack of party discipline but a desire to promote party unity on some issues.

3. The dilemma can be used as a tool to understand both the individual behavior of legislators and the collective behavior of the institution. We are hardly the first to note this relationship. Political scientists Richard Fenno (1978) and David Mayhew (1974, 145–153) have noted the policy and institutional dilemmas, and earlier political philosophers and historians were quite aware of it as well with regard to institutions other than the U.S. Congress. More recently, scholars such as John Aldrich (1995) and Gary Cox and Mathew McCubbins (1993) argue that political parties in Congress were created to solve precisely the types of collective action problems that we outline above. While we agree that parties solve the collective action problem to the extent that they permit Congress to act, we argue that such institutional solutions do not get rid of the basic collective dilemma.

4. Congressional reforms cannot rid the institution of the collective dilemma. This core argument of the book is outlined in the next section and developed more fully in Chapters 4 and 5.

Congressional Reform?

From its beginning, Congress has been the crucible in which basic concepts of U.S. democratic government were hammered out, with many disputes arising over precisely the question of how to reconcile national interests, or the "public good," with local interests and opinions. The collective dilemma framework also draws attention to central disputes of competing visions of representation. The early republic struggled with the question of instructions (in which localities debated the merits of determining how their representatives should vote and so instructed them) versus the concept of "trusteeship" (in which members were held accountable through elections). The relationship between legislatures and alternative forums for representation (the democratic-republican societies of the late eighteenth century, whose modern equivalent is the electronic town hall) is another ongoing debate. A trustee model of representation in a republic such as the United States would favor responsibility over responsiveness, while a delegate model of representation or a direct democracy would favor responsiveness to local concerns.

The relative permanence of this debate indicates that any discussion of congressional reform must recognize that the tension between individual and institutional interests and between the local and the general is inherent and fundamentally irresoluble. Ultimately, we argue, it is simply not possible to "have it all" on both dimensions simultaneously: a legislature can be fully representative, or it can be fully efficient at serving the national interest, or it can be a little of both. Congress may either organize itself to grant legislators the autonomy to act as independent entrepreneurs, or it may create strong leadership structures that tie members to central policies, but it cannot do both at the same time. There is, we conclude, no way to create a legislature that is simultaneously fully representative and fully efficient as a national policymaker, or a legislature that is simultaneously hierarchically controlled while allowing for member autonomy. No matter where a legislature places itself along this representative-national policy (or local-national) continuum, it is guaranteed that some portion of the electorate will be very unhappy with the result.

The tension between representativeness and efficiency is akin to the difficulties in choosing between other compelling, but often incompatible, political values, including, among others: individual liberty and the collective good of society, economic efficiency and economic and political equality, and majority rule versus protection of minority rights.[3] In our view, it is possible to channel in productive ways the conflicts that arise over these values, and it is often possible to find compromises that seek a middle ground. The American bicameral legislative system was designed to strike a balance, with the House of Representatives closely attuned to public opinion and the Senate more insulated from popular passions (the presidential veto and the Supreme Court are additional checks on the legislature).[4]

There are no complete institutional solutions, however, and reforms that seek to resolve one problem will inevitably make others worse. To give an extreme example, a return to the 1950s-style Congress, with entrenched seniority, concentrated power in committee chairs, and strong parties, would solve some of the collective action problems that we identify with the contemporary Congress. By giving a centralized authority the ability to discipline rank-and-file members and allowing committee chairs to push legislation through or block it, Congress would become more efficient and able—in theory, at least—to enforce a coherent party agenda. Yet this "solution" entails the palpable risk of doing violence to minority rights in the name of efficiency. Indeed, the 1950s Congress, especially the Senate, was notorious for its small number of members who blocked civil rights legislation.

Our assessment of Congress's collective dilemma casts doubt on the notion that reforming the institution will significantly alter public attitudes. Procedural and organizational reforms can mitigate the worst aspects of Congress's collective dilemma, but they cannot eliminate it. The organizational alternatives—which usually entail either increasing the centralization within Congress, or decreasing it—each produce their own set of unintended consequences. Many proposed and enacted reforms, such as term limits, a constitutional amendment to balance the budget, cutting committees and committee staff, and the line item veto, will weaken Congress as an institution rather than provide any relief to the forces that affect the institution.

However, it is possible to identify some changes that would have positive effects, inasmuch as they could increase public confidence in the institution and provide members with some mechanisms for advancing collective interests. Some of the reforms we support, such as campaign finance reform and the use of bipartisan commissions where appropriate, have the potential for success. One other proposal—to *reduce* the openness of many congressional procedures—is offered more as a point of departure for discussion, as we recognize that it has little chance of adoption. Nevertheless, it should raise awareness of the notion that increasing openness (due to the adoption of "sunshine laws" in the 1970s) has had some unintended consequences.

Chapter Outline

Our argument is both historical and theoretical. In Chapter 1 we document the nature and depth of the public's disillusionment with Congress as an institution, as well as the large differences between the public's evaluation of Congress (generally negative) and its evaluations of individual legislators (generally very positive). We then describe the policy and institutional dilemmas in terms of a "soft" version of rational choice theory that draws upon economic theories of collective action and applies this logic to congressional behavior. Our particular concern is with individual behavior that demonstrably hurts the institution, as well as with the tension between local representation and national policymaking.

To support our contention that the collective dilemma is an enduring feature of representative institutions, in Chapter 2 we offer evidence that the tensions of the modern Congress have in fact been present from the beginning of the Republic. There are clear parallels—as the 1816 pay raise controversy demonstrates—between public attitudes and congressional behavior in the 1980s and 1990s, with attitudes and behaviors in the eighteenth and nineteenth centuries. Moreover, we also introduce some comparative evidence that legislatures in other countries are experiencing the same sorts of problems that currently beset Congress. The similarities in the problems that legislatures face and the persistence of negative public evaluations, across both time and geography, suggest strongly that the collective dilemma is a basic feature of representative governments. We also introduce historical evidence that the forces we identify have shaped congressional member behavior from the outset and before Congress came into being: Many of the criticisms now leveled at Congress are similar to those made against the Continental Congress and even against the British Parliament in the seventeenth and eighteenth centuries.(The term *lobbyist* originated from the practice of interested individuals making their case in the anteroom of the House of Commons in the seventeenth century.) (Safire 1976, 383).

In Chapter 3 we discuss the institutional and policy dilemmas in the contemporary context. Although we argue that there are strong historical continuities, changes in the past few decades have aggravated the incentives that push individual legislators toward collectively irrational behavior. As modern technologies, such as television and direct mail, free members more than ever from the need to rely on centralizing institutions and organizations (chiefly political parties), the forces that bind members together have become weaker at the same time that the demands on the institution have grown ever greater. Norms that once rounded off the hard edges of the legislative process—deference, seniority, committee influence, collegiality—have eroded, making it more acceptable for members of Congress to engage in the sort of public partisan bickering that puts off the public. Moreover, Congress is an increasingly public and open institution, with more access points and visibility. Bismarck may have been correct when he said, "Laws are like sausages. It's better not to see them being made."

In Chapter 4 we address previous efforts at congressional reform. The collective dilemma framework points strongly to the conclusion that Congress needs mechanisms that facilitate the making of collective policy *and* changes that give members more of a stake in the institution's health and legitimacy. The enduring nature of the dilemma, more importantly, suggests that reform is an ongoing process not a single-shot effort to "fix" the institution once and for all. All congressional reforms—the establishment of standing committees in the early nineteenth century, the adoption of Reed's rules in the 1880s, the revolt against Speaker Joe Cannon in 1913, the Legislative Reform Act of 1946, the legislative reforms of the 1970s, and the new rules adopted by the 104th Congress—were designed to either make Congress a more centralized and structured institution, thus giving more weight to collective decisionmaking capabilities, or to decentralize power and allow members more freedom to pursue their political and/or policy interests. Although some reform periods lasted longer than others, at some point all of the reform efforts fell short in their attempts to cure the collective dilemma.

In the concluding chapter we argue that there are no simple fixes for the characteristics of representative institutions that lead to the collective dilemma. The collective dilemma is not the product of dim-witted or corrupt legislators or of a poorly informed and apathetic public. It is a basic and inherent feature of representative political institutions in which politicians attempt to transform diverse interests and beliefs into majoritarian policies. That task is never easy.

1

Why Don't We Like Congress?

The Collective Dilemma Defined

O ne of the long-standing puzzles concerning the U. S. Congress is why Americans seem to love their own representatives while at the same time detesting the institution of Congress (Fenno 1975). In this chapter we outline the contours of this odd disparity in attitudes and explain it in terms of the collective dilemma that was briefly defined in the introduction. This collective dilemma can be understood in terms of other collective action problems, such as the prisoner's dilemma and the tragedy of the commons, which we explain more fully below. In each of these cases, individuals acting in their own self-interest produce collective outcomes that are preferred by nobody. This, we argue, explains in part why Congress is held in such low esteem.

Public Attitudes Toward Congress

It is no exaggeration to say unequivocally that the public does not like Congress. Public approval of Congress has rarely risen above 50 percent in the last sixty years, which is as long as it has been possible to measure public opinion with any accuracy, averaging about 48 percent approval between 1939 and 1977 (Parker 1981, 32) and less than 40 percent since then (see Figure 1.1). More ominously, Congress's approval rating often dips to what would be considered a dismal level for any other public figure or institution. The lowest approval rating ever recorded for a president was Richard Nixon's 23 percent approval, in an August 1974 Gallup Poll taken just after he resigned. Jimmy Carter's approval rating never dipped below 28 percent, even in the midst of the Iranian hostage crisis and the economic hardships of 1979–1980. Even more astounding was Bill Clinton's approval rating, which remained in the low- to mid–60 percent range early in 1999, even after the impeachment process drew to a close. Congress, in contrast, has routinely enjoyed approval ratings in the mid- to low–20 percent range, with an ABC/*Washington Post* poll recording only 17 percent approval in April 1992.

Although it is commonly argued that Congress is less popular than ever, recent data and scholarship show that this is not necessarily so (indeed, we argue in Chapter 2 that Congress has *always* been unpopular). In Figure 1.1, we plot the

16

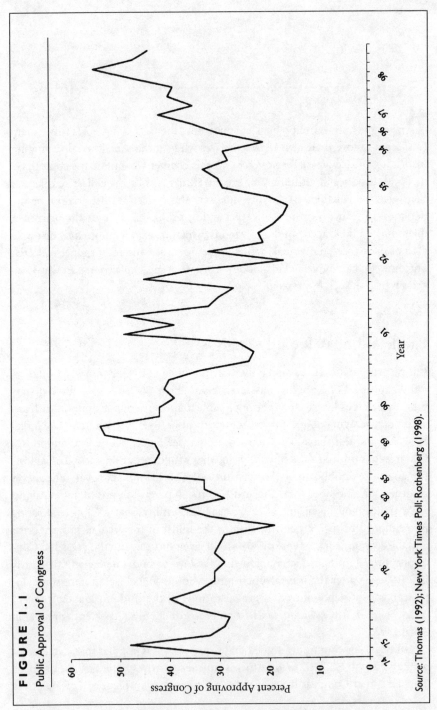

Source: Thomas (1992); New York Times Poll; Rothenberg (1998).

FIGURE 1.1

Public Approval of Congress

Percent Approving of Congress

Year

results of various public opinion polls since 1974 that have asked people whether they approve or disapprove of how Congress is handling its job. Most of the time, public approval ranges between 20 and 40 percent, and breaks 50 percent only a few times during this twenty-four-year period. It is clear that approval ratings have not dropped significantly during this time. This conclusion is also consistent with the results of a recent comprehensive investigation into why the public dislikes Congress, in which the authors disputed the notion that Congress was ever popular. "The evidence that Congress was once liked is weak . . . approval of Congress has never been consistently high, occasionally blipping up but never remaining there for anything approaching a sustained period" (Hibbing and Thiess-Morse 1995, 149).

Why is Congress so unpopular? Many contemporary accounts argue that it is because Congress is fundamentally corrupt and inefficient, and that legislators as a group are dishonest, incompetent, quarrelsome, and more interested in self-aggrandizement than solving problems. A more charitable explanation is that members want to do the right thing but are handcuffed in their efforts by archaic procedures, an entrenched and ossified congressional elite, and partisan wrangling. Tim Penny, a former Democratic representative from Minnesota, lamented the difficulties he faced while in Congress: "I can't tell you how many times in twelve years of Congress, I sat awake at night wondering to myself, Why are we doing these things? Why are so many decent and honorable public servants so incapable of acting responsibly on the central issues of our day?" (Penny and Garrett 1995, 15).

Hibbing and Thiess-Morse argue that the public dislikes Congress because of an aversion to the nuts-and-bolts of the legislative process: "Congress, embodies practically everything Americans dislike about politics. It is large and therefore ponderous; it operates in a presidential system and is therefore independent and powerful; it is open and therefore disputes are played out for all to see; it is based on compromise and therefore reminds people of the disturbing fact that most issues do not have right answers. Much of what the public dislikes about Congress is endemic to what a legislature is. Its perceived inefficiencies and inequities are there for all to see" (1995, 60).

Political scientists have long noted a peculiar characteristic of public attitudes toward Congress, and it is this feature that makes the collective dilemma framework a useful strategy for studying the institution: even though the public may hate Congress, most people are quite fond of their *own* legislator. This dichotomy is at the heart of the collective dilemma concept because it gives legislators a strong incentive to dissociate themselves from the institution of which they are a part.

Figure 1.2 graphs the percentage of the public that approves of Congress along with the percentage of these same respondents who approve of the job their *own* representative is doing. These data are from the National Election Study, a long-running survey of voters conducted every two years. Two patterns stand out. First, individual legislators are far more popular in their constituencies than Congress is as a whole. Over the 1980–1996 period, the average approval rating for Congress was 45 percent, while the average approval rating for legislators was 86 percent. This is continuing affirmation of what Fenno found several decades ago (1975).

The second notable feature of Figure 1.2 is that public ratings of Congress vary more widely than constituency ratings of incumbents. Approval ratings for individual incumbents are steady, ranging between 81 and 91 percent. Approval ratings for Congress are much more variable, moving between a low of 33 percent in 1992 to highs of over 60 percent in 1984 and 1988. Something, obviously, is affecting public attitudes toward the institution, but not attitudes toward incumbents.

This discrepancy between attitudes toward Congress as an institution and toward one's own representative arises because respondents apply different standards when they are evaluating Congress versus individual legislators. When people assess their representative's performance, they consider district interests, the level of contact they may have had with the person, district service (including casework), and the incumbent's personal characteristics (Parker 1981). Members work particularly hard on their "home style" (Fenno 1978) to cultivate a personal connection to constituents.

While constituents, therefore, tend to have some sort of personal affection for their own representatives, Congress as an institution is more removed and abstract (Hibbing and Thiess-Morse 1995). Fenno argues that most people simply "find it hard or impossible to think about Congress as an institution" (1978, 245). When people evaluate *Congress's* performance, they are more likely to think in terms of how well it appears to be meeting public challenges, or the collective performance of all of the legislature's members acting together (Hibbing and Thiess-Morse 1995).

Charles O. Jones, a highly regarded scholar of the presidency, argues that when people are asked about whether they approve or disapprove of the president's performance, what they hear is "How are things going?" (Jones 1994, 118). When the economy is growing, and inflation and unemployment are low, crime is low, and so forth, presidents are more likely to be popular than during wars or recessions. Public evaluations of the president are, in part, based on how things are going in the country as a whole.

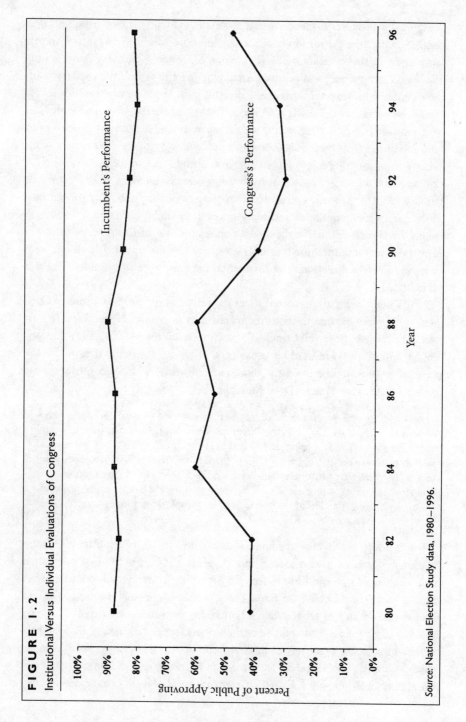

FIGURE 1.2

Institutional Versus Individual Evaluations of Congress

Incumbent's Performance

Congress's Performance

Percent of Public Approving

100%
90%
80%
70%
60%
50%
40%
30%
20%
10%
0%

80   82   84   86   88   90   92   94   96

Year

Source: National Election Study data, 1980–1996.

Figure 1.3 provides evidence that the same holds true for Congress, and that people evaluate the institution based in part on how the country is faring. In this figure, we plot survey data on public approval of Congress, along with the results of another survey question asking people whether they think the country is on the right track or headed in the wrong direction; the series we plot is the percentage of the public that says the country is on the right track. The similarities between the series are striking: on the whole, when the public judges the country to be going in the right direction—a measure of public attitudes toward a *collective* evaluation—Congress enjoys higher approval ratings. One of the highest congressional approval ratings in the past twenty-five years, 55 percent, was measured in January 1998, in the same poll in which 61 percent of the public said the country was generally going in the right direction (itself the highest level on this index in twenty-five years). Similarly, the *lowest* public approval of Congress occurred in April 1992, at the same time that only 16 percent of the public said things were going in the right direction. The correlation between the two variables over this period is .81.[1]

The evidence we have presented so far suggests that public evaluations of Congress are affected by broader assessments of how the country is doing and (by inference) a sense of how well Congress as a whole is addressing the country's problems. Evaluations of individual legislators, however, are more affected by the personal relationship between the representative and his or her constituents. As former Senator Fred Harris (D–N. Mex.) put it:

> People expect their own representative to be their advocate, to speak for them, to represent their interests. This *representation* function of Congress is performed by and large through individual members. Constituents believe that their own member of Congress does a pretty good job at this (perhaps the representatives do a pretty good job of convincing constituents that they are doing a pretty good job). On the other hand, people expect Congress to solve national problems. Solving national problems is the *lawmaking* function of Congress, and most people do not think Congress does very well at it (Harris 1995, 8).

This is not to say that the one has nothing to do with the other. If there were no relationship at all between institutional evaluations and individual ones, then members would have nothing to fear from bashing Congress without mercy because doing so would have no impact at all on their personal political fortunes. But the two are in fact related. Even though people who disapprove of Congress are more likely than not to approve of their own representative, they are less likely to view him or her positively than those who approve of Congress. In 1996, as Table 1.1 shows, the National Election Study found an overall congressional approval of only 33 percent, and an 81 percent approval of one's own representative.

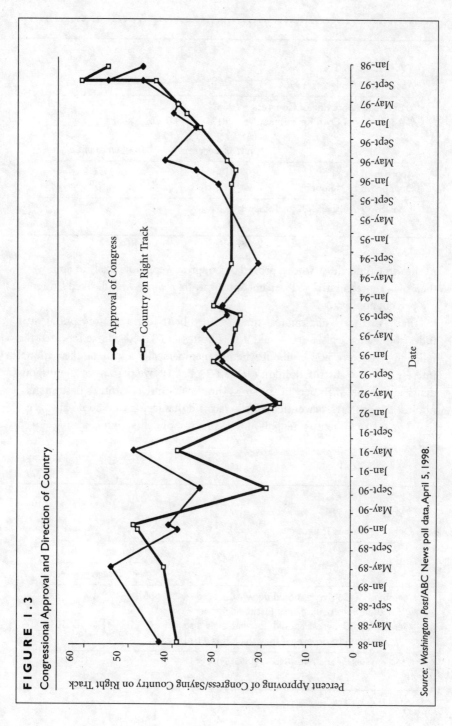

FIGURE 1.3

Congressional Approval and Direction of Country

Percent Approving of Congress/Saying Country on Right Track

Date

◆ Approval of Congress

□ Country on Right Track

Source: Washington Post/ABC News poll data, April 5, 1998.

TABLE 1.1

Approval of Congress, 1996

% of Public Approving of Congress	33%	
% Approving of Own Representative	81%	

	Approve of Congress	*Disapprove of Congress*
Approve of Member	91%	76%
Disapprove of Member	9%	24%

Source: 1996 National Election Study data.

At the same time, those who approved of Congress were more likely to approve of their own representative (91 percent approval) than those who disliked Congress (76 percent approval).

Finally, members of Congress must face explicitly contradictory public attitudes about how legislators should act. Hibbing and Thiess-Morse reported the following survey responses about whether members should pursue the national interest or follow district opinion (Table 1.2). Eighty-five percent of the respondents agreed that members of Congress should act in the country's best interest, not just the district's. Fewer than one in ten said that legislators should always act based on district interests. Yet half of the same respondents *simultaneously* agreed

TABLE 1.2

Delegates Versus Trustees

	Percent of Public		
	Agree	*Disagree*	*Neutral*
Members of Congress should do what is best for the entire country, not just their district	85%	9%	6%
Members of Congress should do what their district wants them to do even if they think it is a bad idea	49%	41%	10%

Source: Hibbing and Thiess-Morse (1995, 64).

that members should do what their district wants, even if the legislator thinks doing so is a bad idea. So, a majority of the public expects legislators to act simultaneously to faithfully reflect district interests and pursue the public good, even if it conflicts with district interests. This presents no problems when district interests coincide with what is in the national interest, but it puts members in an impossible situation when the two conflict (as will often be the case).

These discrepancies in public opinion—the different standards applied to individual legislators and to the institution of Congress and the contradictory attitudes about how members should behave—are at the heart of the collective dilemma concept. They are central because they provide members of Congress with a perfect opportunity to protect themselves. The problem, though, is that in furthering and protecting their own interests, members often behave in ways that have a demonstrably harmful effect on Congress as a whole. To understand why this is so, we discuss the formal theory of collective dilemmas.

The Theory of Collective Dilemmas

Our argument that Congress is beset by a collective dilemma begins with a basic description of the "rational actor" model from economics. We then explain how this model has been used to understand problems in political science. In setting out the rational actor model of individual behavior, our intent is to make some initial and relatively modest assumptions about how people behave, and then follow the logical implications of these assumptions to reach some conclusions about what will happen, or how individuals will react, in various sorts of circumstances.

There are, of course, many important differences in how economists use rational actor theory to understand *market* behavior, and how political scientists use the theory to understand *political* or *collective action* behavior. Markets, to give one example, involve questions of supply and demand, cost and price, and preferences for particular goods. Political arenas, in contrast, involve questions of value preferences, interests, and the connection between individual and group decision-making. Nevertheless, it is quite possible to apply the techniques of economic reasoning to obtain a perspective on how political institutions operate.

The core of economic reasoning is the axiom that individuals are rational utility maximizers. Rational utility maximization requires several assumptions about individual behavior. First, individuals must have a clear idea of what their *interest*, or utility, is on any particular question or decision. It is often easiest to think of this utility in monetary terms, as that is generally the easiest yardstick to measure.

Other things being equal, rational individuals will prefer more money to less. Yet utilities can be measured on many nonmonetary dimensions: one may prefer to live in San Diego over Minneapolis, or prefer vanilla ice cream to orange sherbet, even if one is unable to put a specific dollar value on these preferences. A second requirement for utility maximizing is that, given a set of possible courses of action, individuals must be able to determine the impact each choice might have on their utility, and then to *rank* the outcomes according to which makes the greatest contribution toward maximizing one's utility. Third, individuals must *choose* on the basis of their rank-ordering of possible actions, selecting the one that maximizes utility.

Rational individuals have a clear idea of what their interest or utility is, and they take steps to pursue that interest to the maximum extent possible. While there are many manifestations of what is often called the "rational actor" or "rational choice" paradigm, the basic elements are consistent:

> The traditional rational actor is an individual whose behavior springs from individual self-interest and conscious choice. He or she is credited with extensive and clear knowledge of the environment, a well-organized and stable system of preferences, and computational skills that allow the actor to calculate the best choice (given individual preferences) of the alternatives available (Monroe 1991, 4).

In plain language, a rational utility maximizer knows what he or she wants and faced with any set of alternatives, can calculate which option will provide the greatest return on his or her utility.

In both economics and political science, the assumption of individual rationality raises a number of interesting questions about group behavior. The fundamental problem is this: What happens in a *group* of rational individuals, each of whom is intent on pursuing his or her own utility maximizing strategies? In economics the answer, first established by Adam Smith in *The Wealth of Nations* and confirmed by economists since, is that *markets* can create an optimal group outcome. That is, left to its own devices, and subject to some initial conditions, the "invisible hand" of the market—the operation of the laws of supply and demand—ensures that freely conducted transactions between individuals will produce a maximum level of group utility.[2] Rational individuals, acting together, can produce an outcome that is rational for the group: everyone is better off. In this situation, individual rationality leads to collectively rational outcomes.

But not always. In some cases, individuals who act rationally in a group can produce a collective outcome that is decidedly *irrational*, in the sense that none of the individuals prefers the collective outcome. That is, in a group setting it is possible for each member of the group to act according to his or her rational self-interest but with the consequence that the collective result is an outcome that nobody likes. The pursuit of individual rationality produces an irrational result. These situations are known as *collective dilemmas*.

How can collective dilemmas occur? One good way to explain this concept is to consider two classic statements of the phenomenon: the "tragedy of the commons" and the notorious "prisoner's dilemma."

Example: The Tragedy of the Commons

Imagine that you raise sheep in a nineteenth-century New England town and that many other people in the town raise sheep as well. All of you use a common pasture—a commons—on which you all allow your sheep to graze. Your livelihood depends on your ability to keep your sheep well fed, and your fellow shepherds are similarly dependent on their own flocks. The question you face, along with every other farmer, is how to divide up a scarce resource—the grass on the commons—in such a way that everyone gets his or her fair share.

In this situation, individual rationality produces an irrational outcome. As a rational actor intent on maximizing what you earn from raising and selling sheep, you have an incentive to allow your sheep to graze as much as possible on the common pasture and also to increase the size of your flock. The more sheep you have, the more you can sell, and the more they eat, the bigger they get. You maximize your utility by raising and selling as many well-fed sheep as you can. The other shepherds have the same incentive, however, so everyone tries to use as much of the commons as possible; the inevitable outcome is overgrazing and the destruction of the commons, with the result that there is no grass available for anyone. With no grass, your sheep starve, and you are much worse off than you otherwise would have been.

A key element of the problem is that *no matter what the other shepherds do, you are better off using as much of the commons as you can.* If you are the only one to overgraze, you make more money than you would have otherwise by selling more and bigger sheep; you are better off than you would have been if you had not overgrazed. If all of you overgraze, then your sheep eventually starve, but here too you are better off overgrazing as well because your sheep will at least be able to feed until the commons is depleted. Here, a group of individuals in the rational pursuit of their own interest (maximizing the use of the commons) produces an irrational outcome (the destruction of the commons) that nobody prefers.

This is the classic definition of a *collective dilemma*. It occurs when each member of a group rationally maximizes his or her own utility, only to produce a collective outcome that none of the members prefer. As it happens, there are ways around the dilemma, but they generally presuppose some sort of external authority. The shepherds could agree among themselves to limit the number of sheep each can place on the commons, but here everyone has an incentive to cheat by marginally exceeding their allotment. An external enforcement authority—some sort of police force, binding contracts, and so forth—can solve the problem by imposing some kind of penalty on those who overuse their share. As our next example shows, however, communication is a key part of the solution.

Example: The Prisoner's Dilemma

Imagine that you and an accomplice have been arrested for a crime. The police place each of you in an isolation cell, so you cannot communicate with each other. Both you and your accomplice know that unless one of you confesses, the police do not have enough evidence to convict either of you. The police know this also, so they present you with a choice. You can either implicate your accomplice or remain silent, and your accomplice has the same option. If neither of you implicates the other, you both go free. If you implicate your accomplice and he does not implicate you, you go free and receive a reward, and he goes to jail. If your friend implicates you and you remain silent, he goes free and receives a reward, and you go to jail. If both of you implicate each other, then you both go to jail, but you receive a more lenient sentence for cooperating with the authorities.

Each of you therefore has two options—implicate the other, stay silent—producing four possible outcomes, which can be analyzed in a two-by-two table. (See Table 1.3.) In each cell of the table, the first number is your payoff, the second your accomplice's payoff. For the sake of argument, we assign a value of +1 to going free with a reward, 0 to going free with no reward, −2 to going to jail, and −1 to

TABLE 1.3
The Prisoner's Dilemma

		Accomplice	
		Stay Silent	*Implicate*
You	Stay Silent	0, 0	−2, +1
	Implicate	+1, −2	−1, −1

going to jail with a reduced sentence. This is an arbitrary assignment of utility, but it allows us to analyze the incentives and compare them according to a common measure.

What is the likely outcome in this situation? Obviously, the best possible outcome for you and your accomplice is for both of you to keep quiet. Yet the incentive structure of your options ensures that this will not happen (remember that you cannot communicate with each other and that you are a rational utility maximizer). Your thinking and evaluation of the possible payoffs might go something like this: "Let's say I keep quiet. If I do, my accomplice is better off implicating me than keeping quiet as well, since then he receives a reward *and* goes free (payoff –2 for me, +1 for the accomplice), whereas he only goes free if he keeps quiet (payoff 0,0). Therefore, I expect that he will talk. If he talks, then I am better off talking than keeping quiet, since if I keep quiet I go to jail (payoff –2, +1), but if I talk then at least I get a shorter sentence (payoff –1,–1). Therefore it is in my interest to implicate him. If I talk, and he keeps quiet, then *I* go free with a reward and he goes to jail (payoff +1, –2). No matter what he does, *I am always better off talking than remaining silent.*" You know your accomplice, as a rational utility maximizer, is thinking the same way. Therefore, you both talk, producing an outcome (going to jail, albeit with a shorter sentence) that neither one of you would rationally prefer to going free (with or without a reward).[3]

How do these examples relate to Congress? The point of these exercises is not to draw parallels between members of Congress and criminals or barnyard animals, although we note that some congressional observers have in fact made precisely these links. Mark Twain claimed that, "it can probably be shown with facts and figures that there is no distinctly American criminal class except for Congress," and in the late nineteenth century, Henry Adams, grandson of John Adams, recorded the opinion of a cabinet secretary that, "You can't use tact with a Congressman! A Congressman is a hog! You must take a stick and hit him on the snout!" (Adams 1946, 261).

Rather, the connection is that members of Congress face the same sorts of incentives in choosing how to act as the idealized players in either tragedy of the commons and the prisoner's dilemma games. Imagine, for example, that you are a member of Congress who must decide how to allocate your time, how to vote on legislation, or what sort of campaign strategy you will adopt. In each of these activities, you face difficult choices regarding whether your behavior will be shaped by your own self-interest or by your conception of the collective interest. More often than not, we argue, you will opt for self-interest or the interests of your constituents, even when doing so demonstrably conflicts with the general good (the policy dilemma) or when such action damages the institution as a whole (the institutional dilemma). For example, in Congress nearly everybody participates in a campaign finance system that is widely criticized and brings collective condemnation on the institution. However, very few members are willing to "unilaterally disarm" and impose limits on themselves; therefore the entire process that nobody seems to prefer rolls along. Just like the prisoners who both end up going to jail rather than going free or the farmers who collectively ruin the commons, members of Congress produce an outcome that nobody prefers through their individually rational behavior.

In stating this conclusion, we do not see "self-interest" as inherently bad or selfish. Nor do we suggest that legislators will *never* subordinate their self-interest to the needs of the group (although such instances are rare enough to be historically noteworthy). Rather, self-interested behavior is the inevitable and proper consequence of representative legislative systems in which individuals from geographically based districts come together to make decisions as a group.

We conceive of self-interest in *electoral* terms. Although legislators can have a variety of utility structures or goals—the most often cited is the triumvirate of re-election, influence within the institution, and the making of good public policy[4]—re-election must be the primary goal if members are to fulfill other goals. When engaged in most activities—dealing with constituents, writing or co-sponsoring legislation, floor voting, and so forth—members will almost always at least consider what effect a decision might have on their electoral prospects. This is not to say that electoral incentives will be the only consideration—the political science literature has established that members often retain substantial freedom to act as trustees, especially on those issues on which constituents are either poorly informed or lack strong preferences—but they will usually be at least part of members' decision calculus.

The different choices members make can be classified into two categories, as outlined in the introduction: the *institutional* dilemma, relating to the collective action problem of institutional maintenance, and the *policy* dilemma, stemming from the conflicting local-national interest incentives that members often face.

The Institutional Dilemma

Institutions—organizations characterized by internal complexity, boundaries between the institution and the environment, and universalistic procedures (Polsby 1968)—require time and effort to maintain. Institutional maintenance is a classic collective action problem, because everyone has an incentive to "free ride" by depending on other people to bear the costs. In Congress, institutional maintenance requires such things as serving in leadership positions, performing committee work, organizing the legislative process, and ensuring that the institution completes the tasks necessary to keep it functioning and legitimate. These efforts are costly in the sense that they require time and can divert members from the more immediate interest of ensuring their own electoral survival (member and staff time spent managing the floor schedule is time not available for fund-raising, meeting with constituents, or performing case work).

David Mayhew pinpointed the problem in *Congress: The Electoral Connection*:

> The inclination to do anything at all is, of course, minimal; Congress is more fragile than it looks. Yet from the member point of view the maintenance of the institution is a collective good of some importance. What is needed is a system of 'selective incentives' to induce at least some members to work toward keeping the institution in good repair. And it is just such a system that has evolved over the decades. What happens is that prestige and power within the Congress itself are accorded to upholders of the institution; the Capitol Hill pecking order is geared to the needs of institutional maintenance. Members are paid in internal currency for engaging in institutionally protective activities that are beyond or even against their own electoral interests (1974, 145–146).

While Congress has always faced this dilemma, until recently the organizational structures and leadership patterns did place more emphasis on institutional maintenance and protection of Congress's institutional prestige. A common element of these tasks was that they served a critical integrative function, allowing the institution as a whole to focus more on collective tasks than individual ones. "No collective body," concluded a 1992 study of congressional reform, "can function without a core group of those with stature and mandate to lead the rest, moving them from disparate individual choice to collective action" (Mann and Ornstein 1992, 11).

Yet the incentives to engage in this institutionally protective behavior have declined in recent decades, as have the institutional mechanisms through which those tasks were performed, to the point where it is more and more difficult to engage in the task of maintenance. Even the congressional leadership engages in behavior that harms the institution. The individual incentives that members face push them to slight the institution. The result—a decline in Congress's prestige—is something that few of them would prefer, but such is the nature of the collective dilemma.

To understand how members can behave this way, we can reconfigure the tragedy of the commons problem as follows. Instead of belonging to a group of shepherds who rely on a common pasture for feeding sheep, you belong to Congress, and the common resource is the institutional prestige of the legislature. Each member has two alternative choices of action: to devote time to his or her campaign and election prospects, or to devote time to the institutional needs of Congress (assuming, for the moment, that the two are mutually exclusive, and that there is no electoral payoff in performing institutional tasks). In this situation, the rational choice for each member is to look after his or her own campaign. Yet if every member does this, then no one assumes the costs of maintaining the organization, and the commons inevitably deteriorates.

As in the tragedy of the commons, you are *always* better off acting in your own self-interest, no matter what the other members do: If other members choose to assume institutional duties, you have more time to campaign than they do *and* you benefit from the institutional prestige that the others maintain. If no other member assumes institutional duties, you are still better off if you do the same, since otherwise you are paying the full cost of taking care of the institution and hinder your own electoral duties.

This is more than a theoretical possibility. There is substantial evidence that members do, in fact, sacrifice the institutional commons as they seek to further their own rational interests.

Lack of Time Devoted to Institutional Maintenance

Although there is no shortage of individuals who seek leadership or key committee positions, there is, at least anecdotally, evidence that rank-and-file members are devoting less time to institutional duties. One reason is simply the time pressure that members must deal with, which leaves too little time for substantive duties such as committee work, organizational meetings, and attending floor debates. A second reason is that members appear to be less likely to see their own interests as coincident with the institution's, even in the long run.

Members have too much to do and too little time in which to do it. They are thus forced to make choices about how to apportion their time, and generally choose to put their district and electoral needs before Congress's institutional needs. A survey of members conducted in 1993 for the Joint Committee on the Organization of Congress found that the four tasks members most wanted to spend more time on were studying legislative issues, following floor debate, committee work, and legislative oversight of administrative agencies. The four tasks members were *least* interested in doing more of were fund-raising, giving speeches outside the district or state, meeting with constituents in Washington, D.C., and managing their offices (U.S. Congress 1993, 281–287).

A 1992 Brookings Institution/American Enterprise Institute discussion of congressional reform elicited the following comments from legislators (Mann and Ornstein 1992):

I think you need to start first with what you are trying to accomplish, and you are trying to accomplish a congressional product, an institutional product. Give some of
your time to Congress. We don't expect you to give up your independence or to give
up your district or to give up your need to get reelected. All those are important objectives that you need to carry out as a member of Congress, but at least give us a little bit of time for Congress itself. That is what is really lost around here (2).

There is never any discussion in this place of the obligation of a member to the institution, and if people talk about it, they are embarrassed (4).

The theme expressed here is that members are less inclined to devote any time to
the institution or their own institutional duties. A corollary is that as members are
less connected to the institution as a collective body, they are more likely to "bash"
it for their own electoral and political benefit. While these pressures have always
been present, broader forces inside and outside of Congress have exacerbated
them. Members who care only, or mostly, about their own electoral survival are
not likely to show much concern for the needs of Congress as an institution. "It is
not too much to say that if all members did nothing but pursue their electoral
goals, Congress would decay or collapse" (Mayhew 1974, 141).

The decline in public approval of Congress as an institution is reflected back on
the individual members, putting them in a situation where they are working harder
to maintain membership in an increasingly disreputable club. The benefits of being
a legislator decline, while the costs—both personal and professional—go up. Facing
this set of payoffs, to return to the game-theoretic language, more and more legislators decide that it is just not worth the trouble, and retire. (Of course, members often "retire" rather than face a difficult re-election battle.) It is also becoming harder
to recruit candidates to run for Congress. Increasingly, both parties are finding it
difficult to field challengers, even against potentially weak incumbents. The reasons
are varied—the time and effort of campaigning, the reluctance to endure the fund-
raising necessary to mount a credible campaign, the unwillingness of experienced
state and local politicians to give up their current jobs—but a common theme is
that being in Congress is just not worth the sacrifices involved (Berke 1998, 1).

Running for Congress by Running Against Congress

In 1988, Representative Newt Gingrich (R–Ga.) wrote that the 100th Congress
(1987–1988) had "become the most unrepresentative and corrupt of the modern
era." Accusing it of approaching a "despotic institution," Gingrich characterized
it as "an imperial Congress reigned over by an imperial Speaker" (1988, *ix–x*).
Although Congress has often been the target of such opprobrium, Gingrich's

comments were remarkably harsh, particularly coming from an incumbent with leadership aspirations. (Gingrich became Minority Whip in March 1989, and Speaker when the Republicans won a majority in 1994.)

In criticizing Congress, Gingrich was continuing an American political tradition: the phenomenon of legislators and challengers bashing Congress as an institution is so well established that it has become an iron law of politics. As we noted in the introduction, when Richard Fenno first identified this tendency even among incumbents, he expressed complete surprise, because the strategy appears to contradict basic notions of collective accountability and responsible party government. Fenno's surprise comes from the fact that, on its face, running against Congress "violates every syllable of what political scientists . . . have long taken to be the overarching norm of the House—institutional loyalty. According to this norm, members are supposed to value the House as an institution and do nothing to diminish its prestige or demean its members" (Fenno 1978, 167).

Hibbing and Thiess-Morse also tie the low opinion of Congress to the behavior of politicians: to them, the problem is the public's failure to appreciate the "ugliness of democracy. And no wonder. Politicians are not anxious to tell them. Who runs for office by emphasizing his ability to bargain and compromise? Who runs by saying that the problems are really difficult and that true solutions are probably nonexistent? Who runs by saying she is going to emphasize debate and deliberation? Who runs by emphasizing the extent to which the public is divided on key issues?" (1995, 157).

The Rewards of Leadership: From Institutional Prestige to Involuntary Retirement and Legal Bills

The selective incentives awarded to institutional leaders—prestige, internal power, and respect from colleagues—have changed. Whereas leadership positions were once a perquisite of power granted to senior (and electorally secure) legislators, they now are viewed by voters with suspicion. People who view their own representative as more interested in gaining prestige than in solving problems are likely to disapprove of him or her. As Table 1.4 indicates, of those respondents who said the incumbent was interested in solving problems, 94 percent approved of the incumbent's performance. Where people see the incumbent as more self-interested, approval plummets. Of those who say the incumbent is more interested in gaining prestige, only 53 percent approve of that incumbent.

While those occupying leadership positions often come from "safe" districts—House Majority Whip Richard Armey (R–Tex.) won in 1994 and 1996 with comfortable margins of 76 percent and 74 percent, respectively—seniority offers no

TABLE 1.4

Incumbent Is More Interested in Solving Problems or Gaining Prestige

Approve/Disapprove of Incumbent	Solving Problems	Gaining Prestige
Approve	94%	53%
Disapprove	6%	47%

Source: National Election Study 1994.

guarantee. After becoming Minority Whip in 1989, Gingrich faced his closest election contest ever, winning in 1990 by less than 1,000 votes against an opponent he outspent five to one. When Tom Foley (D–Wash.) lost to George Nethercutt in 1994, he became the first sitting Speaker to lose an election since the Civil War. Gingrich's close call and Foley's defeat occurred in large part because of public perceptions that they were more concerned with national politics than local representation. After Foley received an alarmingly low 35 percent of the vote in an open primary in 1994, his campaign "tried to show that the 15-term incumbent was still listening to his constituents and that, as Speaker, he had the power to amplify the response" (Duncan and Lawrence 1995, 1406). For Foley, though, the effort was too little and too late.

Particularly in the House, those who assume leadership positions are more likely to see their reward come in the form of ethics charges filed against them by the opposition party than as internal prestige. Congressman Newt Gingrich pressed for an ethics investigation into then-Speaker Jim Wright (D–Tex.), eventually leading to Wright's resignation in 1989. Democrats responded by filing a series of ethics charges against Gingrich, who, after assuming the speakership, reversed himself on accepting a multimillion-dollar advance for a series of books. In the 104th Congress, *all* of the top leaders in the House—Speaker Gingrich, Majority Leader Armey (Tex.), Majority Whip Tom DeLay (Tex.), Minority Leader Richard Gephardt (Mo.), and Minority Whip David Bonior (Mich.)—had ethics charges filed against them, as did Rules Committee Chair Gerald Solomon (N. Y.) (U.S. Congress 1997).

After Gingrich resigned his post after the 1998 midterm elections, because of the G.O.P.'s poor showing at the polls, House Republicans chose Bob Livingston (R–Ala.) as their new Speaker. Livingston's reward was to have his own career ruined when it was revealed that he had engaged in several extramarital affairs. As the House was debating articles of impeachment against President Clinton, the allegations prompted Livingston to announce that he would refuse to serve as Speaker and would resign his seat in 1999.

While we certainly are not arguing that Congress should ignore misconduct in office, it is worth noting that ethics charges and investigations are exploding, with more members investigated and sanctioned in the past fifteen years than "in the entire previous history of the institution" (Thompson 1995, 1), at the same time that "most informed observers of the institution believe that the legislators' integrity and competence are greater than in the past" (Thompson 1995, 3).

There are institutional consequences to using ethics charges as an instrument of political warfare. Ginsberg and Shefter have termed this part of a broader pattern of "institutional combat," or the tendency for politics to "center on the efforts of competing forces to strengthen the institutions they control while undermining those dominated by their opponents," a pattern that "undermines the governing capacities of the nation's institutions" (1990, 161).

And while the recent ethics charges vary in their severity, some are indisputably absurd. In December 1995, Representative Robert Torricelli (D–N.J.) filed an ethics complaint against Representative Dick Zimmer (R–N.J.), alleging that a press release issued by Zimmer's office (with the headline "Zimmer Wallops Torricelli in N.J. Congressional Softball Tourney") attacked him in a personal way and violated the rules governing the congressional frank. Zimmer responded that the press release "was a lighthearted description of a congressional softball tournament among the New Jersey delegation" with no personal references. After an investigation, the committee dismissed the complaint as having no merit (U.S. Congress 1997, 22–23).

The same day that Torricelli filed his complaint, he was charged with an ethics violation of his own for issuing a press release that criticized Congressman Zimmer. At the time, Zimmer and Torricelli were both preparing to run against each other for the Senate seat left open by Bill Bradley's (D–N.J.) retirement; the campaign, which the 1998 *Almanac of American Politics* described as "furious" (Barone and Ujifusa 1998, 90), featured harsh attacks from each candidate about ethical lapses by the other. In this instance, though, the Ethics Committee found that Torricelli's press release did in fact violate the rules governing the use of official resources. With evident sarcasm, Torricelli wrote a $2.83 check to the U.S. Treasury "for the cost of four sheets of paper and the use of my office fax machine" (U.S. Congress 1997, 22).

Episodes such as these have two consequences. First, by raising the equivalent of playground spats to formal proceedings, they trivialize the ethics process. In

Reprinted with permission. © Wiley Miller/ dist. by the *Washington Post* Writers Group.

doing so, they clearly undermine the legitimacy of the Ethics Committee, and make it harder to distinguish the truly serious ethical problems from the petty and insignificant ones. Second, there is no question that they divert members from more pressing duties. When a nontrivial number of the "best and most gifted legislators" spend their time on ethics investigations, "Congress weakens its own capacity to do its main job" (Mann and Ornstein 1993, 9) The collective dilemma is clearly in effect: When members file ethics charges against their colleagues for partisan or trivial reasons, they may achieve some immediate gain but it comes at the expense of the institution's reputation and ability to fulfill the lawmaking function.

The Policy Dilemma

In addition to the incentive to attend to their own electoral and political needs at the expense of institutional maintenance, members have a second dilemma: how to balance the "collective good" of the public against the parochial interests of their constituents. This tension arises from the dual nature of Congress as a representative as well as a lawmaking institution and is, we argue, even less amenable to resolution than the institutional dilemma we have just outlined.

Returning once again to the tragedy of the commons game, we can illustrate the dilemma using a classic description of distributive budget politics. In this case, the commons is the budget itself and the decision each member faces is how much spending to claim for his or her district and how much to contribute to the budget in the form of tax revenue from the district. Here, each legislator has an incentive to take as much as possible from the budget, and contribute as little as possible to it, to maximize the net benefits to the constituency. Yet that individually rational decision leads to an absurdly irrational collective result, because it produces at the extreme a budget with infinite expenditures and zero revenue. No matter what the other representatives do, you are better off with a minimal district contribution and a maximum district extraction. To be sure, this is an extreme case, but it does highlight a fundamental distinction between the local and the collective interest in policy. The key is that what may be a rational policy preference for an individual member acting in his or her own interest may not be what is in the interest of the whole. It is a basic dilemma of democratic representative government: should a legislator represent his or her constituents, or the entire polity?

This dilemma arose early in the history of representative legislatures. Edmund Burke, an elected member of the British House of Commons, was the first to state the problem with precision. Writing in the eighteenth century, Burke articulated a vision of representation in which legislators had a responsibility to serve as *trustees*, using their judgment to serve the best collective interests of the polity, rather than as *delegates* whose role is simply to reflect the views of the constituencies that elected them. He expressed this view in the famous *Speech to the Electors of Bristol*, which he delivered upon his election to Parliament in 1774. It bears quoting at length:

> To deliver an opinion is the right of all men; that of constituents is a weighty and respectable opinion, which a representative . . . ought always most seriously to consider. But authoritative instructions, mandates issued, which the member is bound blindly and implicitly to obey, to vote, and to argue for, though contrary to the clearest convictions of his judgment and conscience—these are things utterly unknown to the laws of this land, and which arise from a fundamental mistake of the whole order and tenor of our constitution.
>
> Parliament is not a congress of ambassadors from different and hostile interests, which interests each must maintain, as an agent and advocate, against other agents and advocates; but Parliament is a *deliberate* assembly of *one* nation, with *one* interest, that of the whole—where not local purposes, not local prejudices, ought to guide, but the general good, resulting from the general reason of the whole. You choose a member, indeed; but when you have chosen him, he is not a member of Bristol, but he is a member of *Parliament*.

This theory requires that local constituencies recognize that their representative may not always act to further their own localized interests. Yet not even a politician and thinker as gifted as Burke could strike the requisite balance between his role as a trustee and his constituents' expectation that their views would be represented. By 1780, Burke's constituents had soured on him to the point where he was forced to move to another district to maintain his seat in Parliament.

The problem of how to reconcile local and national interests has been central to democratic political theory. Most of the solutions that have been offered have either presumed the existence of a consensus on what constituted the public good, or sought to put some distance between public opinion and the legislative process. To John Stuart Mill, writing in the nineteenth century, the task of representation was fundamentally different from the task of legislation. The function of representation, in Mill's view, was to provide a platform for the discussion of issues, granting the electorate a forum in which their views could be heard (as reflected by their representatives). But such "talking," he wrote, was very different from the role of *doing* (or legislating), and he argued that popular legislatures excelled at the former but performed dismally at the latter (1910, 240). Representative legislatures should serve to give the public a voice in government, but the task of writing laws and making policy should be insulated from public opinion in order to best promote the public good. In taking this position, Mill echoed the Burkean sentiment that lawmaking should result from deliberation and an expert assessment of what the general good required, not from brokering among competing interests.

Mill suggested that the task of actually writing laws and making policy should be reserved to a "Commission on Legislation," a committee appointed by the Crown, which would "embody the element of intelligence in their construction"(1910, 237). The Commission would write laws and propose them, with Parliament having the power of approval or disapproval. Mill, therefore, separated the lawmaking (efficiency) and representation functions of legislatures into two interlocking, but distinct, institutions. One would be representative, whereas the other, a chamber not connected directly to public opinion and elections, would make laws.

We find similar expressions of dismay over a representative institution's general inability to operate collectively among American political scientists. In a critique of legislative systems written in 1921, historian James Bryce argued that elected representatives may be chosen on the basis of (1) constituent service and promotion of local interests, (2) high character and good judgment, or (3) a willingness to faithfully reflect majority opinion among constituents. It is possible, concluded Bryce, that a legislator could simultaneously serve as a delegate and promote local interests, but impossible for legislators to serve local and national interests at the same time: "No man can serve two masters. Cases arise in which the demands of a locality or the commands of party are at variance with the interests of the nation, and the honest man who perceives this variance will have to sacrifice one or the other" (1921, 352). Similarly, a 1941 committee of the American Political Science Association, formed to study Congress's role during times of national emergency, concluded that "it has always been difficult for a member of Congress to take an overall view of the interests of the country has a whole. The interests of his district or section are likely to be paramount with him, for he depends on their support for re-election" (APSA 1942, 1095).

Members are dependent on their constituents for their political fortunes, so when local interests run counter to what is arguably in the "public interest," we would expect the local pressures to dominate. In addition, when faced with attentive and organized interests balanced against a relatively inattentive public (or on issues where the constituency has weak or nonexistent preferences), we expect Congress to be responsive to those interests. This is why, concludes R. Douglas Arnold, "Congress erects trade barriers to protect specific industries, creates an endless stream of special tax provisions, maintains price supports for many agricultural commodities, and refuses to enact restrictions on the ownership of guns" (Arnold 1990, 3). These are all examples of "distributive policies," or policies that have concentrated benefits and widely distributed costs. In such cases, those who want the benefit have every incentive to organize and fight for it, while the broader and more diffuse population that pays the cost has less of an incentive to organize in opposition.

It is easy to identify policies that reward specific, narrow constituencies without producing much in the way of a general good. Some of the examples involve small programs, such as the federal subsidy to ranchers who raised mohair sheep, a program started in 1954 when mohair was considered a strategic resource because it was used in military uniforms. At its peak, the program cost $200 million per year, and benefited only a few thousand ranchers. By the 1980s, the program had long outlived its original purpose, and wool was no longer critical to the military. A bill to kill the program was introduced in 1983, but it was not until 1993, after paroxysms of congressional effort, that Congress finally ended the program.

The collective dilemma arises when this kind of program proliferates. The result of each member protecting the interests of his or her constituency, at least on budget matters, is spending that is higher than any member might prefer. An illustration of how this arises on a larger program—and which offers an understanding of how legislators find their way out of the distributive morass—is the history of efforts to close military bases (this discussion is taken largely from Mayer 1995).

Military bases are a classic example of a collective dilemma (Cox and McCubbins 1993, 86). Individual legislators who rationally pursue their own interest want to protect bases in their districts, even though the collective result of that behavior—a bloated and costly base system—is something none of them prefers. Members fight particularly hard for their bases, because a closure can eliminate tens of thousands of jobs and cause severe economic contraction. The conventional wisdom held that base closures ended congressional careers, and few legislators were willing to sacrifice themselves.

Yet by the 1980s it had become clear, even to legislators, that the military base structure bordered on the preposterous, and nobody could argue that every base was essential to national security. Some of the more egregious examples of waste were Ft. Douglas, an army post established in 1862 to protect Pony Express mail routes, which eventually wound up in the middle of the University of Utah campus, and Ft. Sheridan, north of Chicago on Lake Michigan, whose chief feature was one of the best military golf courses in the United States. The costs of retaining obsolete bases had become increasingly obvious (Arnold 1990, 140), and the Department of Defense (DoD) wanted to close unneeded bases to free money for other higher priority programs.

But despite the almost unanimous agreement on the need to close bases, Congress had for years erected one barrier after another to prevent any closures: requirements that DoD announce when it was even considering shutting down a base, prohibitions on expending funds to study the savings from closing a particular base, and insisting that the DoD prepare an environmental impact statement on all proposed closures (which, because of the inevitable litigation, would delay the closure for years). Between 1979 and 1985, DoD gave up altogether and did not even attempt to close any bases. Legislators who represented base-heavy districts fought fiercely to protect local jobs and resources, while the general benefits of base closings—lower defense budgets and a more efficient defense infrastructure—were too amorphous to generate much enthusiasm.

It is possible, of course, to push this rational choice argument too far. In the extreme case, as we noted above, we could argue that individual legislators have every incentive to obtain unlimited expenditures for their own districts, while simultaneously refusing to absorb the costs. This would produce an infinite federal budget and budget deficit.

Moreover, Congress *does* legislate in the national interest, and *has* created general benefits at the expense of localized and concentrated interests. Recent examples include the 1986 tax reform law, in which tax deductions and loopholes were eliminated in order to lower marginal tax rates; the base closing laws in 1988, 1990, and 1993, through which DoD closed hundreds of installations, including many large bases; and the 1997 balanced budget agreement, which in fiscal year 1998 produced (unexpectedly) the first budget surplus in thirty years. Yet the impression certainly exists that Congress is better at providing narrowly targeted benefits than it is at general benefits, and examples of individual members sacrificing their political interests in order to achieve a collective policy are rare.

One recent example is the vote that Representative Marjorie Margolies-Mezvinsky (D–Pa.) cast in 1993 in favor of President Clinton's budget and tax package. After prolonged White House lobbying, Margolies-Mezvinsky provided the decisive vote that gave Clinton a 218–216 victory in the House. "She had just gotten off the telephone with Clinton, who told her, in no uncertain terms, that he needed to have her vote. There was only one problem: her career" (Cloud 1993, 225). As the first Democrat elected from her district in seventy-six years, she had promised not to vote for any tax increases. House Republicans, anticipating that the vote would come back to haunt her, were seen chanting "Goodbye, Marjorie" as she voted. She lost in 1994, because she was "unable to overcome from her pivotal vote" on the budget reconciliation bill (Kaplan and Gruenwald 1994, 3239).

This tension between representation and collective lawmaking is, we stress, an inherent part of representative legislatures. It stems from the fact that what is good for individual members is not necessarily good for the institution, or for the "collective good." Yet far from presenting this in a negative light, we see it as an inevitable aspect of democratic governance. To bolster our contention that the collective dilemma is inherent, in Chapter 2 we present evidence that the dilemma has existed in Congress from the earliest days of the Republic and arises in other legislative settings as well.

2

The Collective Dilemma Through History

If we are correct in arguing that the collective dilemma is an inherent part of representative government, it should be possible to view the dilemma in other historical contexts, as well as in other countries with their own forms of democratic government. If, on the other hand, the dilemma is peculiar to late-twentieth-century American politics—or, if it is the consequence of the unique institutional characteristics of Congress, or of venal and demagogic legislators—then there should be eras in which legislators have overcome it. While the nuances of member behavior and criticism of Congress will vary, of course, depending on historical circumstance and the character of individual members, we should at a minimum find evidence that the local-national tension not only has been a consistent theme in congressional behavior, but also has been reflected in how individual members have balanced the needs of the institution against the needs of their constituents. Moreover, we should at a minimum find strong evidence that congressional criticism has been a consistent pattern throughout U.S. history and that it has been independent of the details of different political eras or institutional structures within Congress.[1]

Our review of historical and comparative data supports the argument that the collective dilemma is a constant. The tension between collective behavior in the institution and public interest, and the self-interest of legislators who rely on the support of localized electoral constituencies, is present in virtually every type of legislature. We see it throughout the history of the U.S. Congress, in the state legislatures of the colonial era, and in the British House of Commons of the sixteenth and twentieth centuries.[2] The problem is general, as we noted in the previous chapter. In an open and democratic system of representative government, as long as disagreement exists about what, exactly, the public good is, there will always be tension between local representation and collective lawmaking.

In particular, in this chapter we challenge the notion that the Congress now is a fundamentally different political entity than it was earlier in U.S. history. Despite dramatic changes in the level of institutionalization, size, member professionalism, and electoral structures, members of Congress have *always* faced the local versus national dilemma, or the tension between constituency representation and lawmaking for the general good. Our position is at odds with the received wisdom in contemporary accounts of Congress, which suggest that the institution has strayed far from what the Framers intended and from what the early Congresses did. "Contrary to the expectations of the Founding Fathers," wrote Hammond and Wyerich (1988, 237) in a sharp criticism, "the House of Representatives has become a self-perpetuating oligarchy in which the political choices of a majority of Americans have been offset by an elaborate system of electoral jury-rigging, and in which the interests of a few districts predominate in the decisionmaking process. The Senate is moving in the direction of the House, but more slowly."

Once again, we emphasize that we are *not* arguing that Congress has never been able to pass legislation that created general public benefits. At times, Congress has even taken the lead on the question of the public good, only to be rebuffed by the president or the courts. But that is the exception.

The Framers' Views of the Local-National Dilemma

No one has devised a strategy—theoretical or otherwise—that resolves the dilemma between local and national interests. Virtually every political theorist who has considered the question has, in effect, admitted that the two functions of lawmaking and representation cannot easily be combined. The compromises that went into the initial structure of Congress—bicameralism, a popularly elected House with a Senate chosen by state legislatures, a small size compared to the existing state assemblies, longer terms for Senators—reflected an attempt to reconcile the competing interests in accordance with republican principles, but even the Framers found that they were overly optimistic in their hope that local or sectional interests would give way to a broader concern with national well-being.

For the most part, the Framers solved the collective action problem by assuming that in the new Republic, factional pressures would be mitigated through the election of "men who would be able to pursue vigorously what they saw to be the true interest of the country free from the turbulence and clamors of 'men of factious tempers, of local prejudices, or of sinister designs'" (Wood 1969, 505, citing Madison's October 24, 1787, letter to Thomas Jefferson). A core of the argument Madison set out in *Federalist* 10 is that larger constituencies would be more likely to focus on national issues, and smaller constituencies to show undue concern with local interests. In making this argument, Madison was strongly influenced by what he saw as the narrow and parochial concerns of state legislatures. Elkins and McKitrick (1993, 702) described the prevailing view of state houses as places where the public good was continually trumped by provincialism, "all amid a babel of contending local demands, selfish private and parochial interests, and the pushing and shoving demagoguery of popular politics."

How did the Framers see Congress? Although they were concerned with the notion of representation—even though their ideas of *who* should be represented differed from more modern views—they very clearly demonstrated a concern with the *national* good over local interests. In *Federalist* 56, for example, Madison avowed that "it is a sound and important principle that the representative ought to be acquainted with the interests and circumstances of his constituents," and the two-year House term was specifically intended to tie legislators to public sentiment. At the same time, the *Federalist* made it quite clear that the new government was by no means a direct democracy that would put all questions of policy to the public. In *Federalist* 57, Madison pursued this line of thinking, setting forth the proposition that "the aim of every political constitution is, or ought to be, first to obtain for rulers men who possess most wisdom to discern, and most virtue to pursue, the common good of society."

The debates between the Federalists and Anti-Federalists (who opposed the ratification of the new Constitution) reflect this tension between national and local interests. The Anti-Federalists emphatically denied that the new Congress would be able to overcome local interests in order to maintain national well-being, or even that this would be a good thing. One Anti-Federalist writer, James Winthrop of Massachusetts, argued that "it is vain to tell us that we ought to overlook local interests. It is only by protecting local interests that the interest of the whole is preserved" (cited in Kenyon 1955, 9). We note that even Madison expressed some contradictory attitudes about the relationship between local and national interests. Although he saw Congress as the mechanism for pursuing collective interests, in *Federalist* 51 he noted the centrality of individual interests to preserving limits on government power: that "the private interest of every individual may be a sentinel over the public rights."

In *Federalist* 10 and 51 we see the emphasis on countering the long-standing notion that republican governments are impossible in large and diverse societies. In contrast to the Anti-Federalist argument that only a small and homogenous nation could be ruled by republican principles, Madison sought to convert that liability into an asset: by arguing that diversity of interests, itself brought about by large size and heterogeneity in the body politic, would prevent a cohesive majority from forming and running roughshod over minority rights. "It is no less certain than it is important," wrote Madison in *Federalist* 51, "notwithstanding the contrary opinions which have been entertained, that the larger the society, provided it lie within a practicable sphere, the more duly capable it will be of self-government."

What historical evidence is there for the existence of the collective dilemma in Congress? We argue that it is simply that the same sorts of criticisms and behavior that critics find in the contemporary Congress have been present throughout congressional history.

The Policy Dilemma in the Early Congresses: Parochialism Versus the National Good

Although our historical memory serves up images of great statesmen in the first Congress delivering utterly persuasive orations about what the new country needed, in fact the opposite was true: the new legislature was dominated by patterns of compromise, local concerns, negotiation, the occasional stalemate, and a number of blunt debates between political foes. More to the point, all this occurred even as the institutional prestige of the new Congress would have a direct bearing on the immediate survival of the new constitutional structure. If the institution simply could not fill the role for which it was designed, its failure would undermine the foundations of government. To their dismay, however, the Framers' hopes that Congress would be guided by a dispassionate pursuit of the public good fell apart almost immediately, as sectional and partisan interests arose over almost every issue that Congress considered. Sharp (1993, 33) reports that James Madison's initial enthusiasm for what he "perceived as a lack of sectional and state friction" in the first Congress was destroyed by the end of 1791, in which "bitterness, rancor, and fear for the union" had replaced earlier optimism. The collective dilemma emerged immediately, as legislators found it close to impossible to suppress constituent interests in the name of the general welfare.

The first order of business taken up by the newly convened Congress was the question of how the new government would finance its operations. There was broad agreement about the need for revenue, as well as a consensus in favor of raising the revenue from tariffs and imposts on imported goods. Yet despite the existence of this common ground, and with the new Congress still in the shadow of the Constitutional Convention and ratification, the "national good" gave way to concerns over which goods should be taxed, and by how much, with the opinions of the legislators determined largely by the interests of their particular regions. The following exchange on April 9, 1789 (*the first day that Congress convened*), between Madison and Thomas Tudor Tucker, a Congressman from South Carolina, captures the pressures that members faced:

> Tucker: How meddle with what may dissatisfy our constituents? . . . Where different interests prevail it is supposed that different sentiments will arise, and gentlemen from those states which interested with a heavy tonnage duty be inclined more favor-

ably than those from other states which wish lighter or no duty at all, and be for a measure that others may be against—and not altogether consistent with the general good.

Madison: I am sensible great weight in what fell from gentleman from South Carolina. Necessary to weigh and regard the sentiments of gentlemen from different parts of the United States. But on the other hand we must limit our consideration by considering the national import as well as state import. This is founded on the ideal of mutual concession (Bickford et al. 1992, 10–12).

Tariffs, once seen solely as a neutral mechanism for raising revenues, evolved into an instrument for the protection of local industries, and legislators sought to use the tariff bill to protect newly developed industries in their home states, which would be hurt by less-expensive British imports (Elkins and McKitrick 1993, 65). Representatives from Pennsylvania sought tariffs on iron, steel, and saddlery products, "all of which happened to be produced in respectable quantities in the state of Pennsylvania (Elkins and McKitrick 1993, 66).

Senate in 1850. Courtesy of the Library of Congress.

Fisher Ames, a senator from Pennsylvania, who was one of the more vocal critics of the early Congresses, enthusiastically participated in this process of protecting local interests. Ames worked hard to *prevent* high tariffs on molasses, which was imported into Massachusetts in large amounts and used to make rum and other products. High prices for molasses, Ames warned, would cause families to go without their treasured sweetener and undermine the legitimacy of the nascent legislature. "Mothers will tell their children, when they solicit their daily and accustomed nutriment, that the new laws forbid them the use of it, and they will grow up in a detestation of the hand which proscribes their innocent food and the occupation of their fathers" (cited in Elkins and McKitrick 1993, 66).

By 1791, Madison was lamenting the parochialism of congressional decision-making, expressing sorrow that

> it almost always happened, whenever any question of general [good] and advantage to the Union was before the House, when gentlemen found themselves at a loss for general arguments, they commonly resorted to local views; and at all times, as well as the present, when there was most occasion for members to act with the utmost coolness, when their judgments ought to be the least biased—it was to be regretted that at those times they suffered the feelings, passions, and prejudices, to govern their reason. Thus it is, that the most important points are embarrassed, the Northern and Southern interests are held up, every local circumstance comes into view, and every idea of liberality and candor is banished. (History of Congress December 1791, 266)

Other members expressed similar disappointment at the degree to which Congress deferred to constituency interests. Of these early Congresses, Pierce Butler, a senator from North Carolina, found

> locality and partiality reign as much in our Supreme Legislature as they could in a county court or State legislature. Never was a man more egregiously disappointed than I am. I came here full of hopes that the greatest liberality would be exercised; that the consideration of the *whole*, and the general good, would take the place of every other object; but here I find men scrambling for partial advantages, State interests, and in short, a train of those narrow, impolitic measures that must, after a while, shake the Union to its very foundation. (cited in Harlow 1917, 138)

Logrolling and parochialism played a role in even the most critical issues. Northerners, according to Howard Ohline, backed away from an effort in 1790 to act on a formal report that was harshly critical of slavery (the Foster Report). Because they were concerned that action would alienate Southern legislators and therefore hurt efforts to resolve the issue of assumption of state war debts, antislavery forces refused to press the issue; in taking this position, the Northerners were reacting to the "immediate pressure of special-interest politics" (Ohline 1980, 355).

The frustration with the *processes* of legislation in the early Congress is neatly captured by the contemporary account of Louis-Guillaume Otto, France's chargé d'affaires in the United States from 1785 to 1791. Otto was a close observer of the second congressional session, which met from January to August 1790, and he recorded his impressions in detailed correspondence with the French Minister for Foreign Affairs (O'Dwyer 1964). The main issue in the second Congress was the question of assumption of Revolutionary War debts, and the agenda was set largely by Alexander Hamilton's Report on Public Credit. When Congress first took up the question of assumption, Otto wrote on February 25, 1790, that "the debates of the House of Representatives are becoming daily more interesting. The public flocks there in crowds to hear the interests most dear to the nation decided" (O'Dwyer 1964, 420).

But the debate over assumption and finance proved unexpectedly difficult to resolve. Over time, Otto expressed more and more frustration with the process, complaining in July that it was only by accident that the public good resulted from the intrigue and selfishness that he observed: "[A]s it is impossible to deceive an entire nation about its true interests, it generally happens that the private egoism concentrated in that of the nation leads to an honorable end by means which are hardly so and by men who desire the good only because it is personally useful to them" (O'Dwyer 1964, 439). In assessing the government's performance, Otto contrasted the "president's responsibility and good judgment" with that of the legislature, "which, not being responsible for anything, always includes a large number of intriguers and mediocre persons" (O'Dwyer 1964, 443).

The difficulties of reconciling local interests and the national good persisted through the nineteenth century. Congress struggled repeatedly with the task of setting tariffs, which continued to be the primary means of raising revenues until the income tax was established in 1913. Tariffs invariably pitted different interests and regions against each other: agriculture versus industry, cities versus the frontier, North versus South. Similarly, different regions approached internal improvements (roads, bridges, canals) with varied enthusiasm depending on how badly they needed these early public works projects. New England states tended to have an adequate infrastructure and preferred to handle improvements themselves. The South, fearful of increasing federal government involvement and its implications for slavery, was also unenthusiastic (Swift 1996, 104–108). These sectional disputes were reflected within Congress, with legislators unsuccessfully attempting to balance, in particular, the interests of the South with an increasingly vocal antislavery coalition.

To summarize, the picture of the early Congress as a legislature consumed with promoting the collective good is false. From the beginning, members grappled with the question of how to balance constituent interests against the national interest, and more often than not they failed to meet the Framers' hopes. "The Founders' expectations that the diversity of the country with its multiplicity of interests and divisions could be overcome by a selfless elite acting in the national public interest," concluded James Rogers Sharp, "were to be profoundly disappointed and frustrated" (1993, 34).

Interest Group Politics

Although "lobbies"—organized groups that attempt to persuade legislators and mobilize supporters—did not exist in eighteenth-century U.S. politics,[3] Congress *did* face routine requests for legislative action through public pressure. In this regard the new Congress was "remarkably sensitive to popular opinion" (Rakove 1987, 292). "Within days of his election," wrote historian Jack Rakove (1987, 289), "Madison began receiving the first of a stream of requests for federal patronage."

Public pressure on Congress was exercised mainly through petitions or written requests for specific legislative action. The practice, which was "the most widespread means for popular participation in the political process" in the first few Congresses, served as a vital link between constituents and their representatives (U.S. Congress 1986, 6). There were, according to the most comprehensive count available, 1,887 such requests submitted between March 1789 and December 1795 (U.S. Congress 1986, 362). Most petitions requested what would now be called a "private bill," or requests for individual relief, and usually dealt with pensions for Revolutionary War veterans and their survivors or claims for property damaged or confiscated during the war.

A significant number of petitions, however, were submitted by groups clearly asking for "special interest" legislation. Between March and September 1789, for example, the 1st Congress received nine petitions requesting that federal offices be located in specific cities, four petitions asking that duties on imports be raised in order to protect domestic producers, nine requests for legislation to promote the shipping industry, and eighteen petitions asking Congress to grant individuals exclusive rights to particular inventions or publications. Over the next year, Congress received petitions from individuals and groups asking for government insurance for the payment of war debts (with many of these petitions originating with groups holding securities, and thus with a direct economic stake in debt legislation), military contracts, construction of harbor improvements and naval hospitals, and one petition asking for a subsidy for malt liquor producers (U.S. Congress 1986, 16–128). These requests were equivalent to modern supplications for tax breaks, local construction projects, and regulatory favors, all the type of legislative action that infuriates critics of congressional profligacy or special interest favors. The quaint nature of many of these petitions is a function of the government's limited powers: without significant responsibility, there was only so much the government could do, and thus little motivation for pressure groups to organize. Even so, in those areas where Congress was competent to act, constituents were not afraid to ask for favors.

Like their twentieth-century counterparts, legislators in the eighteenth and nineteenth centuries grew weary of devoting so much time to casework and constituency service. In 1815, a House member from Massachusetts complained that "I have been constantly engaged in attending to some private business for my constituents and friends, who think they have a right to call on me for that purpose." An Ohio Representative weighed in similarly in 1816: "I never was more industriously engaged than in attending to the private business of others" (both citations from Cunningham 1978, 987). While serving in the House in 1831–1832, James K. Polk kept meticulous records of his constituency service activities. "His ideals were not very elevated," according to a review of these records, "but such as they were he never shirked them. To attend to the little necessities of his constituents exactly comported with his ideal of a congressman's duty" (Bassett 1922, 69).

The history of colonial legislatures suggests a connection between the level of institutionalization of a representative institution and the degree of "organized" constituent pressure that would be brought to bear on it. Around 1700, for example, the major colonial legislatures (Virginia, Pennsylvania, and Massachusetts) had such informal procedures that even members were often unsure what laws they had enacted: laws were not codified, procedures for publicizing laws were slipshod, and constituents often felt justified in simply ignoring laws they opposed. Although, Olson concludes, these legislatures attempted to show responsiveness to constituent demands, they faced few outside pressures because "procedures were so unsystematic that constituents were not sure how their concerns would be handled; the publicity for assembly decisions, once made, was so limited that constituents were not always sure how their concerns *had* been handled," and as a consequence, people simply took their concerns elsewhere for redress, either going above the assemblies to Parliament or relying on local institutions (Olson 1992, 550).

Ultimately, concludes Rakove, the Framers erred in their hopes that the new government would focus on the general good; this was, he argues, a direct consequence of the way that they wrote and promoted the Constitution. The public campaign for ratification ushered in an era of popular politics, and "the idea that the deliberations of Congress could be safely insulated from interests and pressures arising within the states and individual constituencies was one of the casualties" of this process (Rakove 1987, 294).

There are direct links between the failure of the Framers' designs and modern criticism of Congress. Contemporary critics often argue that Congress's failure to act in the public interest—and, we note, there is often sharp disagreement about what, exactly, the public interest is—reflects an institutional failure. If only members would set aside their ambitions and petty political biases, the thinking goes, surely they would be able to assess accurately the country's real problems and to figure out what to do about them. Lani Guinier, who has written extensively about representation and minority interests, sees jury deliberations as the model for effective representation. When juries consider the evidence in a trial, they must "put aside their biases, deliberating only on the basis of the evidence. Their mission is to review the evidence and decide an outcome that is in the public interest, rather than in their self-interest" (Guinier 1994, 107).

Guinier articulated a long-standing vision of legislative deliberation, and one perfectly consistent with what the Framers hoped to create. Moreover, her argument is comparable not only to the Framers' ideal but also to the argument made by Henry Butler, an M.P. in the nineteenth century. In a public letter written in 1809, Butler criticized Parliament for deviating from its original function, which was "to *represent* [the people], to speak their opinions, and to act their will . . . it was never in the contemplation of our ancestors that any motive but the public good would ever influence a majority of their representatives" (Butler 1809, 4).[4]

But, as Alan Brinkley (1997, 26) has persuasively argued, this is a seductive but ultimately chimerical notion:

> The belief that a pure "public interest" exists somewhere as a kernel of true knowledge untainted by politics or parochialism, and that it provides not just an array of basic principles but a concrete set of solutions to complex problems, is an attractive thought, but it is also a myth. We may be able to agree on a broad framework of beliefs capable of organizing our political life, but any such framework will have to make room within it for conflicting concepts of how to translate those beliefs into practice.

Public Disillusionment with Congress

Dissatisfaction with legislatures was widespread in the colonial period, despite the fact that the colonial assemblies produced a period in which "the people . . . had never been more fully and fairly represented in any legislatures in their history" (Wood 1969, 328). Nevertheless, charges of poor representation spurred the development of numerous alternative practices and institutions, such as conventions or informal congresses, which were seen as even better mirrors of public will (Wood 1969, 328–329). By the 1780s, with a few years of experience with the Articles of Confederation, there was "scarcely a newspaper, pamphlet, or sermon . . . that does not dwell on this breakdown between the people-at-large and their representative governments" (Wood 1969, 368).

Early criticism of Congress tended to break down along ideological lines; this was especially true of newspapers, since most were openly supportive of one or the other of the developing political parties. The Senate, in particular, came under sharp criticism for its secrecy: one writer complained in 1792 that "it augurs an unfriendly disposition in a public body that wishes to masque its transactions— Upright intentions, and upright conduct are not afraid or ashamed of publicity" (cited in Swift 1996, 58). Pressure from public opinion, the press, and several state legislators played a key role in the Senate's decision in 1794 to open its proceedings to the public (Swift 1996, 59).

By the 1820s, Congress—particularly the House—had fallen in the public's regard. Alexis de Tocqueville observed in his *Democracy in America* that "[o]n entering the House of Representatives at Washington, one is struck by the vulgar demeanor of that great assembly. Often there is not a distinguished man in the whole number. Its members are almost all obscure individuals, whose names bring no associations to mind. They are mostly village lawyers, men in trade, or even persons belonging to the lower classes of society. In a country in which education is very general, it is said that the representatives of the people do not always know how to write correctly"(1945, I, 211).

There is little doubt that, by contemporary standards, congressional ethics in the eighteenth and nineteenth centuries left much to be desired. In the 1800s, for example, members routinely took money from companies with a direct stake in legislation and accepted money from individuals in return for handling their claims against the government. Bribery of legislators became a crime only in 1853 (Thompson 1995, 2).[5] Allegations of corruption were common as early as 1790, and the deciding vote on Hamilton's original assumption bill was said to have been purchased by a bribe (MacNeil 1963, 212); whether or not this story is true, there is no disputing that many legislators who voted on the various assumption plans owned debt instruments that would be directly affected by the choice of which plan would be adopted (Kirby 1970, 30). In the notorious Crédit Mobilier scandal of the 1870s, a dozen influential members of the House accepted stock in return for protecting government subsidies to the Union Pacific Railroad and blocking a congressional investigation into the company (Kirby 1970, 31–32). Until the Civil War, dueling was a common method of settling disputes between members, and legislators often came to the floor of the House armed with pistols; firearms were brandished on the floor on more than one occasion in the nineteenth century (MacNeil 1963, 306–307).

Negative public reaction was continuous, and attempts by some to counter the increasingly harsh coverage in the press went nowhere. In 1897, Senator Henry Cabot Lodge (R–Mass.) complained about press coverage of Congress and the long-standing tradition of Congress bashing:

> It is habitual in the newspapers and in conversation to sneer at the debates in Congress, as it is at everything connected with that body. . . . The truth is, that if any one will take the trouble to follow the debates—a privilege which the general public does not now enjoy—he will find that, while there is unquestionably a certain amount of ignorance and cheap talk and empty declamation inseparable from any popular representative assembly, the discussion on the whole is carried on vigorously and effectively, and with a great deal of special information on the many and varied subjects which come before both the Senate and the House (*Nation* 1897, 63).

The magazine *The Nation* would have none of this. It responded to Lodge's remarks by noting

> The reputation of Congress is not based on its oratory, because the public does not hear it. It is based on its conduct as a legislature; and the popular opinion about its oratory is a deduction from its statesmanship. People conclude, perhaps too hastily, that a man who acts like a fool cannot make a good speech. . . . It would not be possible for Congress to sink so low that thousands would not seek seats in it, as long as the salary of Congressman was $5,000 a year. The idea that the place is sought on account of the high reputation of the body approaches perilously near a joke. . . . We have here recalled only a small portion of the things which have exposed Congress to popular contempt, and the remedy is not to write articles saying it is wise and eloquent, but to *be* wise and eloquent. Its career for the last ten years has caused great national despondency and distrust, which cannot be removed by self-praise (*Nation* 1897, 63).

The situation had not improved by 1925, according to House Speaker Nicholas Longworth (R–Ohio):

> I have been a member of the House of Representatives [for] twenty years. . . . During the whole of that time we have been attacked, denounced, despised, hunted, harried, blamed, looked down upon, excoriated, and flayed. . . . From the beginning of the Republic it has been the duty of every free-born voter to look down upon us, and the duty of every free-born humorist to make jokes at us (Kirby 1970, 4).

Finally, for evidence that "objective" indicators of legislative quality have almost nothing to do with how the public views such institutions, we offer the following description of the Alabama State House:

The legislatures of a generation ago . . . were, to put it bluntly, racist, sexist, secretive, boss-ruled, malapportioned and uninformed. But there was no great public outcry against any of those conditions. The Alabama legislature, ranked in a Ford Foundation study in 1971 as 50th out of 50th in independence, 50th in accountability, and 48th in overall performance, had been judged favorably just three years earlier by 65 percent of the respondents to a statewide poll. In 1990, freed of its racism, secrecy, and malapportionment, fully equipped to gather information and operating in a new, state-of-the-art legislative facility, it got an approval rating of 24 percent (Hibbing and Thiess-Morse 1995, 149, citing Alan Ehrenhalt).

This review of public attitudes, while admittedly unsystematic, suggests strongly that dissatisfaction with Congress has more to do with the inherent qualities of the institution than with any peculiarities of how Congress is doing at any given time. It is surely true, as Hibbing and Thiess-Morse concluded in 1995, that a

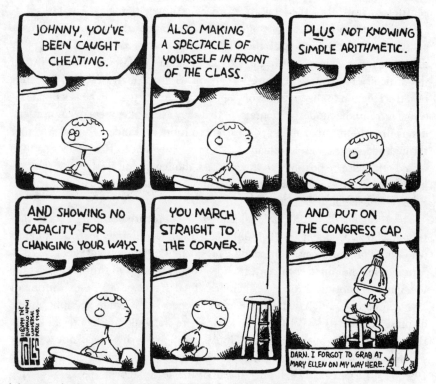

Johnny, you've been caught cheating. TOLES © 1991 & 1997 the *Buffalo News*. Reprinted with permission of UNIVERSAL PRESS SYNDICATE. All rights reserved.

large part of popular discontent with Congress is, has always been, and always will be, "endemic to open democratic government" (1995, 1).

The Institutional Dilemma

It is more difficult to find evidence of the institutional dilemma—or the disincentives to devote time and effort to institutional maintenance—throughout American history, in part because the early Congress lacked many of the institutional characteristics of the modern Congress. At that time, members devoted less time to their institutional duties, mostly because Congress met infrequently, travel to the capital city was difficult, and, most important, turnover was extraordinarily high. Between 1790 and 1834, each election brought at least one-third new membership to the House, and turnover often exceeded 50 percent every two years.

In these first few Congresses, there was no leadership, at least in the form that it exists today: no seniority leaders, no formal organizational positions, and no centralized control of the legislative process (Young 1966, 95). The tasks performed by the modern congressional leadership—organizing the party caucuses, assisting with legislative organization, scheduling, agenda control, enforcing party discipline (such as it is)—were carried out in an ad hoc fashion, if at all. Part of the difficulty in creating effective leadership within Congress was an intensely negative reaction to the very idea of political parties. Parties are the key organizational force in the modern Congress, in that they assign members to committees, determine the number of seats on each committee, bind members together through ideological ties, and help craft a more coherent legislative agenda than would otherwise be possible. To the Framers, though, political parties were nothing more than an especially dangerous form of faction and viewed as anathema to government stability.

There was *informal* congressional leadership, a practice begun by Thomas Jefferson, who as president (1801–1808) worked with certain members of Congress who would promote legislation that the president wanted (Young 1966, 127–135). Throughout the nineteenth century, however, leadership positions (other than the Speaker) continued to exist as "informally designated, indefinite, shifting or even competitive, and based on such factors as personal prestige, speaking ability, or presidential favor" (Polsby 1968, 158). There was little prestige to leadership roles, and the key position in the House, the Speakership, "was not a highly sought-after position and was generally occupied by 'second rate men'" (Palazzolo 1995, 1258). Henry Clay, considered one of the all-time great Speakers (serving for much of the 1811–1824 period), is viewed as enhancing the prestige of the office and establishing it as an independent source of power within the legislature. Even so, notes Polsby, there are questions about whether Clay used the power of the Speakership for policy or institutional purposes, or whether he was mostly interested in furthering his presidential ambitions (Polsby 1968, 156). In the nineteenth century, concluded Swift, apart from a handful of senators who appeared dedicated to their institutional duties, the commitment of most "fell far short of the level . . . the framers had envisioned" (1996, 79).

Running for Congress by Running Against Congress: The Early Years

One thing that is clear is that the practice of running for Congress by running *against* Congress emerged quickly. Congress was not immediately the subject of criticism, either by members or from outside, but the absence of early attacks had more to do with the impression that criticizing government over policy was the sort of factional politics that the Framers worked so hard to avoid, rather than any widespread belief that Congress was doing a good job. Yet once a legitimate opposition developed, something simply not present at the founding, and which arose largely over Secretary of the Treasury Alexander Hamilton's plans for a national bank and an industrial policy, those inside government found it more acceptable to level criticism against Congress itself (Elkins and McKitrick 1993, 263–264). By 1792, Jefferson was complaining to George Washington that Hamilton's financial policies had encouraged rampant speculation, leading to "a Congress 'legislating for their own interests in opposition to those of the people'" (Elkins and McKitrick 1993, 288).

As partisan divisions within Congress solidified, the first signs of members becoming openly critical of the institution became evident. The first member to "run for Congress by running against Congress" was probably Matthew Lyon, a Democratic-Republican from Vermont. Lyon, who first came to Congress in 1797, was immediately derided by Federalists, who considered him crude and boorish. Lyon's opponents mocked his Irish heritage and modest beginnings, and criticized him for using the frank to send circulars and newsletters to his constituents (Smith 1956, 221–223). Lyon's problems worsened in 1798 when he spat on fellow Representative Roger Griswold on the House floor in response to some taunts Griswold had made about an alleged incident during the Revolutionary War. Federalists immediately moved to expel Lyon from the House but failed (*Benton's Abridgement*, 2, 206). Two weeks later, Griswold entered the House floor and beat Lyon with a cane, an incident which led to a motion demanding that both men apologize and pledge "not to commit any act of violence upon each other during this session" (2, 212).

In 1798, in what would lead to proceedings under the Sedition Act, Lyon attacked President John Adams' attempt to secure congressional support for his policy toward France. Lyon quoted from a letter that referred to a "bullying speech of your President, and stupid answer of your Senate," and which concluded that the Senate had "echoed the speech with more servility than ever George III experienced from either House of Parliament" (Wharton 1849, 334; Smith 1956, 227). Based on this incident, in October 1798 Lyon was convicted of publishing seditious libel against President Adams and the Senate, sentenced to four months in jail, and fined $1,000. "For the first time in American history," wrote Smith (1956, 238), "a candidate for Congress conducted his campaign from a federal prison." Yet in a result that would have impressed James Michael Curley, the legendary Boston politician who in 1904 was elected to the Boston City Council while jailed on fraud charges, Lyon easily won re-election, beating his closest Federalist opponent by more than a two-to-one margin (Wharton 1849, 342).

By 1800 legislators had settled into the habit of criticizing the institution and other members. Although there was, of course, less coverage of congressional activity and individual statements in the late eighteenth and early nineteenth centuries, we can still identify themes in the images that legislators presented to their constituents through circular letters that were common at the time. In these letters, which were distributed as general information newsletters in districts or published in newspapers, members were able to communicate with their constituents. And although we do not pretend that the examples we cite are part of a uniform pattern—and note that circulars were almost exclusively from the South—the themes are common enough to suggest that members recognized the advantage they could gain by putting distance between themselves and the institution.[6]

John Fowler (Kentucky), March 4, 1799: "I had foreseen that some active persons, in despight of all that could be urged to prevent it, would be enabled, by their management, to drag others along with them, who, forming a majority, would complete a scheme, the dangerous consequences of which were not duly appreciated" (Cunningham 1978, I, 182).

Thomas T. Davis (Kentucky): "Congress, like all other large bodies that have a variety of interests to reconcile and different opinions to combat, have progressed but slowly in the business before it" (Cunningham 1978, I, 182).

Robert Goodloe Harper (South Carolina), March 5, 1801: "The power of a popular assembly, being little suspected by the people, is always little watched; and as no one member is to bear the blame of any excesses which the whole body may commit, its power is but little restrained by personal responsibility and a regard to character; and of course is very likely to be abused. Hence has resulted, in every age and nation where the form of government admitted popular assemblies, a constant effort, on the part of those assemblies, to get all power into their own hands, and to exercise it according to their own passions and caprice" (Cunningham 1978, I, 253).

John Fowler (Kentucky), March 6, 1801: "The last session of the Sixth Congress closed on the 3d instant, and with it a career of errors and extravagance never before known among us, and rarely exampled any where" (Cunningham 1978, I, 265).

James M. Garnett (Virginia), April 12, 1808: "It is with real regret, I find that my duty both to you and myself, imposes upon me the necessity of appearing so often to blame the conduct of those with whom I act" (Cunningham 1978 II, 562).

Jacob Swope (Virginia), April 28, 1810: "Congress will rise on the first of May, after a protracted session of five months, in which, the conduct of the majority has been marked by folly and indecision. We have passed many laws of a local nature, which I forbear to enumerate, as they have no connection with the interests of my constituents" (Cunningham 1978, II, 701).

Archibald McBryde (North Carolina), May 10, 1810. "At the commencement of the late session of congress, it was well known that many subjects of the greatest national importance would present themselves to the consideration of that body. The critical situation of our foreign affairs, the low and embarrassed state of our revenue, and the great increase in our expenditures, demanded our careful attention: but although we had a session of more than five months, and all these subjects brought in some form before us, very little has been done. I know, however, that this is a matter of consolation to many: If we have done but little good, they give us credit for doing less harm than they once apprehended" (Cunningham 1978, II, 704).

John Stanly (North Carolina), May 10, 1810: "This disgraceful and truly humiliating state of things has been seen with grief & indignation by every intelligent man who has visited the seat of government during the session—And to what source is it to be traced? It is almost exclusively ascribable to that dominance of party spirit, which, conscious of its weakness and jealous of its security, rejects every proposition coming from the minority in Congress, and to the imbecility and want of talents in a great proportion of those who form that majority" (Cunningham 1978, II, 730).

These criticisms of Congress were hardly academic, as at times the basic legitimacy of the new Congress was called into question by opponents who refused to recognize and abide by some of its more controversial acts.

The Collective Dilemma in Other Institutional Settings

The evidence we have offered thus far supports the argument that the collective dilemma has existed throughout congressional history. We see in the Congress of

1800 patterns of parochialism, public disenchantment, constituency pressure, and institutional lethargy that are quite similar to what we observe in the 1990s. Thus, we conclude that the collective dilemma has been consistent across time.

The British House of Commons is in most respects vastly different from the U.S. Congress. Parliament plays a distinctly secondary role to the executive branch, which is itself headed by M.P.s serving as prime minister and in the Cabinet. Members are poorly paid compared to members of Congress: the M.P. salary in 1998 was about $75,000, compared to approximately $133,000 for members of Congress. They have almost no staff: The office and staff allowance for each M.P. in 1997 was just over £47,000, or about $79,000. The average allowance for a member of the House of Representatives that year was $901,000 (Ornstein, Mann, and Malbin 1998, 151). Although the office allowance has grown since the 1980s, when it "fell so far short of [constituency service needs] that it discourages MPs from being conscientious" (Crewe 1985, 46), it still permits no more than a minimal constituency presence. Members of Parliament are almost entirely dependent on parties for their campaign funds, and the amount they can spend on their campaigns is strictly limited (about $12,500 in the 1997 general election). The dependence of members on their parties has given rise to a "textbook" picture of a Parliament of M.P.s as:

> Faceless troops in the party ranks who vote in accord with the party whip. They have little or no personal power (e.g., committee based as in the United States) to procure "pork" for their districts or to provide favors to individual constituents. . . . [T]heir parliamentary careers hinge not only on their continued local renomination and re-election, but also, and more important, on the impressions they make on national party leaders. To cap it all off, their constituents can register a preference for the executive only through their vote decisions for Parliament (Cain, Ferejohn, and Fiorina 1984, 114).

One advantage that the British Parliamentary system is said to have over the United States is that its tradition of very strong parties and unified government (in which the executive offices are all filled by M.P.s from the majority party) greatly simplifies the task of focusing on the *collective* public good rather than local constituency or organized group interests. On the other hand, individual M.P.s have very little opportunity to have an impact on the legislative process, unlike members of the U.S. Congress who have far more autonomy and influence. The ability of British parties to discipline errant members, even to the point where it is possible to prohibit someone from running on the party ticket if leaders disapprove, should, in theory, give members more of an incentive to adhere to the party agenda and make them less likely to simply reflect local interests.

And it does. But our conception of the collective dilemma is that while centralization can *mitigate* the need to focus on local interests; it cannot *eliminate it*. The main feature shared by Congress and the House of Commons is that members are elected from single-member winner-take-all districts. This ensures that members have at least some tie to local interests, and thus creates the dilemma. Despite the strength of party discipline in Britain, M.P.s still focus on activities, such as local representation and casework, that translate into an incumbency advantage and personal connection between constituents and their own M.P. (Cain, Ferejohn and Fiorina 1984). Research on the 1992 British general elections concluded that district-level campaigning improved the electoral performance of Labour and Liberal Democratic candidates, confirming that local efforts make a difference (Denver and Hands 1997).

More important, even with its strong parties, the collective dilemma still exists in Parliament, which struggles with the need to combine local representation with the collective legislative function. Survey research as early as 1966 showed evidence that "constituents expect their Member to put local interests, and local opinion, before all else" (Crewe 1985, 48). The ideal M.P., according to the voting public, is

> a local resident who devotes his full time to the job of dealing with constituency problems and conscientiously attending local meetings; who occasionally sallies forth from the constituency to express his views in the 'national debate' at Westminster; and who in cases of conflict gives precedence to constituents' views over those of party, to the local over the national party, and to the party's before his own (Crewe 1985, 50).

The impact of these outside forces and constituency demands has grown in recent years, as a 1997 report by the Commonwealth Parliamentary Association made clear. "Parliamentarians work under tremendous pressure," the report concluded, "and the demands of their constituents continue to grow. Their duties call for a full-time commitment to both their constituencies and their parliamentary work and without the right facilities they cannot operate effectively" (Laundy 1997, 27–28). In Great Britain, as in the United States, the number of lobbyists and interest group organizations has grown dramatically in recent decades, and M.P.s "are far more vulnerable now than they have been ever before to outside and commercial pressures" (Laundy 1997, 115).

Parliament suffers, in addition, from many of the pathologies that afflict the U.S. Congress. Britons distrust Parliament as much as Americans distrust Congress, perhaps more. In 1995, a Gallup poll found that 77 percent of the British public thought that M.P.s "cared more about special interests than about ordinary people"; 87 percent said that "MPs will tell lies if the truth would hurt them politically"; 64 percent believed "most MPs make a lot of money by using public office improperly" (Leigh and Vullamy 1997, xv). The "hate Congress–love my

TABLE 2.1

Attitudes Toward Politicians in Great Britain

	1944	1972	1979
Politicians are mainly out for themselves	36%	38%	48%
Politicians want to do what's best for the country	36%	28%	18%

Congressperson" dichotomy exists in Great Britain as well. One M.P. put it this way: "As politicians generally we are rated fairly low in people's regard [but] often you find that regard for an individual MP puts them high in the list of public perception within the constituency" (Laundy 1997, 113).

Broader research confirms this view. The public views the ethics and social value of M.P.s as a group to be quite low, ahead of union officials and reporters, but behind doctors, lawyers, and the police. Although the majority think that M.P.s in general "forget about the people who elected them," 98 percent also think that their own M.P. does at least a fair job for his or her constituency (Crewe 1985, 56). This dichotomy arises even though parties retain almost complete control over nominations, and even though the explicit connection between individual M.P.s and their constituents is far weaker than the connection between members of Congress and their districts.

As has happened with Congress, public confidence in Parliament has declined as well. The data in Table 2.1 show that people are much more likely now than in the 1940s to view M.P.s as self-promoting opportunists: A strong party structure, combined with limited individual autonomy, will reduce the impact of the collective dilemma, but it will not eliminate it.

Finally, Hibbing and Thiess-Morse found that dissatisfaction with the legislature has emerged as a consistent pattern in the newly emerging democracies in Eastern Europe. As these former Soviet satellites make the transition from central control to democratic governments, the public does not always like what it sees. Concluded Hibbing and Thiess-Morse:

Residents of the United States are not distinct in their contempt for modern legislative bodies; the attitude is global. it is particularly instructive to see dissatisfaction with national legislatures so prevalent in the new democracies of Central Europe. Public opinion polls in the new democracies show that it is common for people being exposed at close range to democratic procedures for the first time to recoil instinctively, and for them to recoil most from legislatures, since that is where these procedures are most evident (1995, 150).

Again, we interpret these common themes regarding legislative behavior, throughout history and across geographic areas, as evidence that representative legislatures share some fundamental characteristics that are not the result of particular political context, organizational processes, or the characteristics of members. That is not to say, however, that context, organization and members are irrelevant, because they are quite relevant. In Chapter 3, we analyze the relative impact these changes have had on Congress.

3

The Collective Dilemma in the Modern Context

In Chapter 2, we argued that the collective dilemma has existed in Congress throughout the institution's history and also that the dilemma exists in other legislatures. In this regard, the contemporary Congress shows many similarities to its historical predecessors. Yet although legislators have always shown great deference to local and organized interests at the expense of the collective needs of the public, in the view of many the problem has only become worse. The modern Congress is charged with being less concerned with the public good and more attentive to special interests than ever. Journalist Jonathan Rauch (1994) even coined a new term, *demosclerosis*, to describe what he views as an excessive level of responsiveness to interest groups, which he declines to define as "special" since they include almost everybody. Even political scientists (who, as a rule, are more sympathetic toward Congress than either the public or the media) have joined in the criticism. "More than at any other time in the nation's history," argues political scientist Lawrence Dodd,

> Congress is elected and organized to serve the disparate elements of a self-interested public rather than to identify and foster the shared concerns of a public-spirited citizenry. Congress increasingly lacks the ability to recognize the mutual concerns and shared interests of the public, and the ability to discover new governing principles that could resolve our policy dilemmas and renew public faith in government (1993, 418).

To Dodd, Congress has historically served the valuable function of melding disparate opinions into collective decisions that addressed the country's major problems. This deliberative function, he goes on to say, has collapsed in the face of intransigent social and economic problems. The "unique severity, perhaps even the insolubility, of post-industrial problems" of economic stagnation, an increasing gap between the rich and the poor, huge deficits, urban decay and violence, and rapid technological change combine to render Congress powerless, and undercut the institution's legitimacy (Dodd 1993, 422).

Political scientist Dennis Thompson argues that these developments have increased the level of *institutional corruption* in Congress. Institutional corruption is different from *individual corruption*. Individual corruption involves the pursuit of personal gain through political office: soliciting and taking bribes, nepotism, and the like. Institutional corruption, concludes Thompson, arises from behavior in which "the *gain* a member receives is political rather than personal, the *service* the member provides is procedurally improper, and the *connection* between the gain and the service has a tendency to damage the legislature or the democratic process" (Thompson 1995, 7). When Congress regards what should be considered unethical behavior by legislators as part of normal practice, the institution clearly suffers.

Although it is easy to argue that things are "worse" now than they have ever been before, the normative judgments implied in this view obscure important continuities in the history of interest representation in Congress. Do the American Association of Retired Persons, the National Rifle Association, organized labor, or the Association of Trial Lawyers of America hold more sway over Congress in 1998 than did Southern agricultural interests in 1794 or the railroad industry in 1880? Are lobbyists more of a problem now, because of their numbers and financial resources, than they were in 1913, when the National Association of Manufacturers dictated congressional committee assignments, paid the House clerk to record private conversations between members, and had its own offices inside the Capitol? (Luneberg 1998, 7). Is Congress *less* responsive as a lawmaking institution now than it was in the 1790s, when huge numbers of people were barred from voting because of their gender, race, or lack of wealth? Or in the 1880s, when dilatory tactics by the minority made it impossible to conduct even routine business? Or in the 1950s and 1960s, when a House or Senate committee chair could single-handedly derail civil rights, minimum wage, or housing legislation? Were the budget deficits of the 1980s and 1990s or the gap between rich and poor (or the other issues noted by Dodd) more serious crises for the nation than the Civil War or the Great Depression?

In our view, this pessimistic picture of the contemporary Congress is overstated. In part, our assessment of the contemporary criticism is conditioned by the fact that Congress has always been unpopular. The opinion that Congress is worse now than it has ever been thus relies on a rosy picture of what Congress was like in the nineteenth and early twentieth centuries. The specifics of Dodd's criticisms—that Congress cannot respond adequately to contemporary problems, that it is paralyzed by the demands of narrow interests, and that it is unable to forge majoritarian and deliberative policies—in fact restate the arguments of earlier critics who wrote in vastly different economic and political contexts. Whatever the causes, it is not the decline in the stature of senators and representatives alone that is responsible for the decline in Congress's reputation. Consider, for example, what a newspaper editorial had to say about Congress in 1837, when Henry Clay, Daniel Webster, and John C. Calhoun (three of the greatest members in congressional history, and known as the "Great Triumvirate") served in Congress: "A more weak, bigoted, persecuting, and intolerant set of instruments of malice and every hateful passion, were never assembled in a legislative capacity in any age or any land" (Wiley 1947, 6).

In 1922 Walter Lippmann traced public dissatisfaction with Congress to legislators' lack of knowledge. "The main reason for the discredit [of Congress]," wrote Lippmann, "which is world wide, is, I think, to be found in the fact that a Congress of representatives is essentially a group of blind men in a vast, unknown world" (Lippmann 1922, 182). Four years later, in 1926, Representative Robert Luce (D–Mass.) defended Congress against the charge that it was not up to the challenges of modern government:

> Congress suffers most, because there is no place higher up to which it can turn for relief. Its old labors remain while the new ones are added. . . . But the stubborn facts of social and economic change must be accepted. Congress is not to be blamed for them, nor can it fairly be criticized if it has not proved fully equal to the tremendous increase in its responsibilities (Luce 1926, 132–133).

In 1945, a study of congressional organization by the American Political Science Association had this to say about interest groups:

> [A] pressure group economy gives rise to "government by whirlpools" of special-interest groups in which the national welfare is often neglected. This pulling and hauling of powerful pressure groups creates delays and distortions which imperil national safety in wartime and threaten bankruptcy in time of peace (APSA 1945, 73).

Laments over Congress's apparent inability to forge consensus or legislate for the collective good are thus nothing new. However, the argument that "things aren't so bad now, it's *always* been this bad," may not provide much comfort to citizens concerned about inefficiency in government. The next section directly challenges the view that congressional policymaking can best be understood as the service of special interests.

Is Congress in the Pocket of Special Interests?

One reason for the public's low opinion of Congress as an institution is the belief that it "sells out" the collective good in order to protect narrow interests. Although we do not dispute that this criticism is often on target (indeed, our central premise is that for individual legislators this is a perfectly rational outcome of the collective dilemma they face), in many cases the argument oversimplifies the

vastly intricate dynamics of complex legislation. Two brief case studies, on tobacco legislation in 1998 and Clinton's 1993 health care plan, will demonstrate
that understanding the collective dilemma is not as simple as assuming that narrow geographic or special interests will always win out over collective interests.

Smoking Out Tobacco

Our first example concerns 1998 legislation involving the tobacco industry, surely
the archetype of a narrow interest whose fortunes conflict with the public good.
Tobacco is a highly profitable, $170-billion-per-year industry (Greenblatt 1998,
1306), but one accused of peddling a highly addictive and dangerous product.
Forty years of scientific evidence had conclusively linked smoking to deadly disease, including cardiovascular disease, cancer, emphysema, childhood illnesses,
and asthma among nonsmokers who live with smokers. The Federal Government
estimates that smoking-related disease causes 400,000 premature deaths each year
and imposes $100 billion in costs on the American economy. The Environmental
Protection Agency concluded in 1993 that secondhand tobacco smoke was a
"Group A Carcinogen," which put it into the same category as radon and asbestos.
The U.S. Surgeon General, the American Medical Association, the American Psy-
chiatric Association, the Centers for Disease Control and Prevention, the World
Health Organization, and virtually every other medical and public health agency
in the world considered nicotine a highly addictive substance, with physiological
effects similar to those of cocaine, amphetamines, and opiates (Food and Drug
Administration 1995). The industry had no credibility at all with the public: in a
May 1998 poll conducted by the Mellman Group, only 2 percent of the public said
they trusted the tobacco companies "a great deal" on the public heath issues of tobacco use; 48 percent said they didn't trust the industry at all.

In 1994, when industry officials testifying before Congress denied under oath
that nicotine was addictive, they sounded as if they were insisting that the earth
was flat.

Nevertheless, tobacco companies had for decades successfully fought lawsuits
seeking damages from the harmful effects of cigarettes and continued to earn
enormous profits from tobacco sales. Critics—and there were many—claimed
that the industry's success in evading responsibility for its actions stemmed from
large campaign contributions to elected officials (especially legislators) and extensive lobbying. Between January 1979 and April 1998, tobacco-related interests had
contributed over $31 million dollars to federal candidates and political parties. In
1997 alone, the industry spent $19 million on lobbying activities. This hefty level
of activity, claimed the Center for Responsive Politics, paid off in legislation that

provided generous tax breaks and other special considerations to the industry (Center for Responsive Politics 1998). If ever there were an example of money purchasing influence at the expense of the public welfare, this would be it.

But despite this concentration of economic and political power, tobacco's position unraveled in the early 1990s. In May 1994, the Mississippi attorney general sued the major tobacco companies to recover the costs of treating smoking-related illnesses. Thirty-nine more states followed with lawsuits of their own. As part of the discovery process in these lawsuits, the plaintiffs discovered damning internal company documents suggesting that the industry manipulated nicotine levels in cigarettes to keep smokers hooked, intentionally marketed cigarettes to children, and suppressed research on the harmful effects of smoking. In August 1995, the Food and Drug Administration asserted that cigarettes were drug delivery devices, a claim that would give the agency regulatory authority. The industry's "wall of silence" collapsed in March 1997, when one of the companies named in the state lawsuits—the Liggett Group—admitted in a settlement agreement with twenty-two state attorneys general that cigarettes cause cancer, that nicotine is addictive, and that the industry marketed to underage smokers.

It is an understatement to say that these developments severely weakened the industry's legal position and raised the likelihood of ruinously expensive litigation. Of the forty-one lawsuits filed by states, settling the first four cost the industry $36 billion; there were thirty-seven more to go in addition to a potentially endless stream of individual lawsuits. To ward off this possibility, the larger companies agreed to settle the state lawsuits en masse, offering to pay $368 billion over twenty-five years in return for limitations on its future liabilities. From the companies' vantage point, the pressure to obtain liability limits intensified in June 1998 when a jury awarded punitive damages against a cigarette company for the first time. These damages were subsequently overturned on appeal for procedural reasons, but the prospects for mounting liabilities remained very real (Schwartz 1998).

This was where Congress came in. Only Congress has the authority to provide national liability protection, so the tobacco settlement required legislative approval. Congress would have to enact the settlement into law in order for it to take effect. The industry strongly supported the proposed settlement and looked to Congress to provide the relief it sought. This is no doubt a good test of the proposition that a highly motivated, well-financed, and sophisticated lobby can trump broader public considerations.

Despite intense industry lobbying and pressure in favor of the original settlement legislation, the prospects for a neat resolution evaporated when Senator John McCain (R–Ariz.) introduced an alternative bill that was much tougher on the industry. Instead of $368 billion in payments over twenty-five years, the Mc-Cain bill (S. 1415) required $516 billion and provided virtually none of the liability protections the industry wanted. Proponents of increased health expenditures found it easy to raise taxes on cigarettes to pay for a variety of new programs. Mc-Cain's bill raised tobacco taxes by $1.10 per pack, more than quadrupling the then-current tax of $.24 per pack. Another bill reported by the Senate Finance Committee offered even worse terms, with a $1.50 per pack increase. The *Washington Post* described the prevailing wisdom about the astonishing turnaround in tobacco's political clout:

> That the Senate is on the verge of considering such change has amazed political observers familiar with the many ways complicated legislation can find a fatal end in Washington. In this case, the driving force has been an unwavering public disdain for the tobacco industry and growing insistence on some kind of change (Torry 1998).

Support for the bill in the Senate was such that members began loading it down—in "Christmas tree" fashion—with all manner of amendments, some completely unrelated to the original legislation. By mid-June, the Senate had added a tax cut and funding for antidrug programs, and was considering amending the bill to increase hospital stays for women who have mastectomies, and to deny student loans to those convicted of drug offenses. As the bill became laden with extraneous material, opponents began criticizing it as a "tax and spend" bill, and even supporters conceded that the legislation needed to return to its original focus.

When it became clear that Congress would require the industry to pay more to get fewer protections, a group of tobacco companies announced on April 8, 1998, that they would abandon their efforts to devise legislation and fight the bills making their way through the Senate. The industry then embarked on a high-profile, $40 million public campaign to portray S. 1415 as a punitive measure aimed at working people.

In June 1998, the McCain bill died when it could not garner sixty votes to overcome a filibuster. Its defeat was seen as conclusive evidence of the power of narrow interests. "If anyone needs any more proof that big money talks in Washington," argued Common Cause President Ann McBride in a June press release on the tobacco bill, "they need look no further than the debate on the legislation now before the United States Senate." McBride called tobacco industry contributions "nothing less than protection money" and argued that the industry is now "cashing in on its investment by trying to kill the tobacco legislation in the Senate" (McBride 1998).

From the industry's perspective, defeating S. 1415 was certainly preferable to passage, but even defeat left companies no better off than they were before the original settlement agreement. The demise of the McCain bill freed the industry from the need to pay $516 billion, but it also meant no liability protection of any sort. As a result, the industry was vulnerable to the same threat of litigation that drove it to seek relief in the first place. The large campaign contributions, lobbying expenses, and soft money donations undoubtedly helped to ward off S. 1415, but they did not help the industry obtain the legislative protection it wanted, either.

The crucial point here is that the ultimate outcome was driven by John McCain's fight for a tougher bill than the tobacco industry was willing to swallow. As it turns out, it was more than Congress would support as well. However, if Congress were truly in the pocket of the tobacco companies, the first version of the liability protection would have passed. *This was the tobacco companies' preferred position.* Yet they walked away with nothing because one powerful senator decided to fight for the broader public's interest rather than a narrow special interest.

In November 1998, a coalition of state attorneys general proposed a new settlement in their lawsuits against the tobacco industry, with the industry agreeing to pay $206 billion over twenty-five years. This was, to be sure, a better deal than the $368 billion industry payment required in the first version of the tobacco legislation that Congress considered, but it did not offer the same liability protection that Congress would have provided. Individuals could still sue tobacco companies under the state settlement, and the various class action suits would proceed as well (Levin and Weinstein 1998, A1). To the extent that the tobacco industry got off lightly, part of the blame goes to Congress's failure to enact settlement legislation. That failure, though, was not the result of legislators seeking to go easy on the industry, but occurred when they tried to get too tough. Had McCain not offered S. 1415, Congress very likely would have passed the original legislation.

Congress Gets a Bum Rap: The Politics of Health Care Reform

Another example of the complexities of the collective dilemma is the congressional debate over health care reform and the fate of President Clinton's Health Security Act. In September 1993, after months of task force meetings chaired by first lady Hillary Rodham Clinton, the president unveiled legislation to fundamentally restructure health care. Clinton had promised major reforms during the 1992 campaign, and the public was overwhelmingly in favor of significant action. In 1991, Democrat Harris Wofford had won an upset victory in a Pennsylvania Senate election, with health care reform as his central theme. The public pressed for reform out of concern over rapidly rising costs, fears of losing health insurance, and a desire to maintain access to advanced treatments. A September 1993, *Los Angeles Times* poll found that an astounding 92 percent of the public believed the health care system needed at least some improvement, with 50 percent saying that a "fundamental overhaul" was required. Twenty-two percent identified health care as the nation's most important problem, behind only crime (33 percent) and ahead of unemployment, drugs, the deficit, and the economy.[1] Given the overwhelming public support and a strong presidential commitment, this was the most propitious opportunity for comprehensive reform that the nation had seen in decades. Here was a classic case of Congress having an opportunity to further the public good, even if it might hurt the interests that benefited from the existing health care delivery system.

One year later, health care reform was a complete failure: Clinton's plan got nowhere in Congress, never achieving so much as a single floor vote. Numerous alternative proposals from both liberals and conservatives had fractured the initial coalition in favor of the Clinton plan, and public support had nearly evaporated. Strong opposition from small businesses, insurance companies, and other health-related interests helped derail the legislation: on September 26, 1994, Senate Majority Leader George Mitchell (D–Maine) pulled the plug on the ailing patient and declared health care reform dead (Rubin 1994b, 2797).

What happened? There are many explanations for the failure of health care reform, with various accounts attributing it to, among other things, poorly drafted legislation, inadequate efforts to mobilize public support, inconsistent and contradictory public demands, political ineptness on the part of the Clinton administration, distraction over other issues, hubris, and conservative success in tapping into public fears of "big government" and exploding deficits.[2] Journalist James Fallows (1995) faults the Clinton Administration for failing to counter the often inaccurate attacks on the plan.[3]

But a common theme of many critical accounts is that Congress's failure can be traced to the lobbying and campaign contributions of corporations, trade associations, and businesses that opposed Clinton's plan (as exemplified by the notorious "Harry and Louise" ads, financed by a health insurance trade association, in which an average couple fretted about the details of the plan over their kitchen table):

> During 1994, millions of dollars were spent in private advertising to influence the national debate on health reform. Total independent expenditures were greater than the amount spent by both sides in a presidential election. This would present no problem if there had been adequate time, money, and effort to respond. There wasn't. . . . Money gave a minority the power to shape votes in Congress through campaign donations, greatly influenced what information Americans received by large scale spending on advertising, and stacked the deck by putting a large amount of money into mock "grass roots" organizing (Heymann and Heymann 1996, 516–517).

Skocpol (1996, 97–98) argued that many public interest groups—such as the League of Women Voters and the Henry J. Kaiser Foundation—supported the Clinton plan, but as tax-exempt organizations they were legally prohibited from expressly advocating any legislation or making campaign contributions; corporate groups, trade associations, and political action committees faced no such restrictions. Another account argued that the fate of health care reform reflected "the repeated failure of American political institutions to address the polity's problems" which "has worked to undermine dramatically the public's faith in their governmental institutions" (Steinmo and Watts 1995, 365).

The assumption underlying these accounts is that Congress had failed the public, that the debate over health care was distorted by biased lobbying and fake grassroots campaigns, and that this was yet another case of Congress showing too little concern for the public good and too much concern with well-heeled special interests and short-term partisan advantage.

Our focus on the collective dilemma presents a somewhat different interpretation of the health care reform effort. In our view, the demise of the Health Security Act conforms well to what we would expect, given the initial collective dilemma that legislators faced and how events unfolded. Our argument is that although a majority of members initially favored some sort of health care reform (indeed, the conventional wisdom at the time was that the Health Security Act would be relatively noncontroversial), when public support waned as the details of the plan emerged and the tradeoffs became clearer, enough individual legislators saw that it was in their own self-interest to oppose major change that significant reform was doomed. In addition, once public support began to drop, congressional Republicans made a conscious effort to block any significant legislation in the hopes that public disillusionment with Congress would redound to their own advantage (they were correct, and this belief helped them gain majority party control of Congress in 1994). Finally, there is abundant evidence that although the public was critical of Congress's handling of health care reform, they did not hold *individual* legislators at fault and instead focused their disdain on the institution.

Thus, while there is certainly evidence to support the view that special interests helped kill health care reform, there is little doubt that members of Congress were also responding to their constituents who told them, when push came to shove, that they were pretty happy with their health care the way it was. Fear of the unknown became quite apparent as the debate progressed, and members of Congress responded to concerns about what would happen to the quality of care for the 80 percent of Americans who *did* have health care (and who voted more often than the people who were not covered).

Health care legislation clearly presented legislators with an institutional dilemma. Members of Congress acted in their own self-interest (whether in response to the health care industry or their geographic constituents) in killing the legislation, but in doing so contributed to the public's frustration that "Congress can't get anything done." Whether one views the failure of health care reform as a classic example of the collective policy dilemma depends in part on how one defines the collective good that was undermined: If members of Congress defined the public good in terms of the 80 percent who already had coverage, then there was no collective dilemma. If the public good was defined in terms of the 20 percent who were not covered, clearly there was a dilemma. Those who favored the single-payer plan or Clinton's plan would see it as a failure, but those who would prefer market-based approaches and limited government intervention in health care would not. Choosing between these two sides is largely a value judgment.

For confirmation that legislators were beset by contrasting forces, we begin with evidence that at least initially a majority of legislators, both Republican and Democrat, _favored_ some sort of comprehensive health care reform (although not necessarily the Clinton plan specifically). Both Democratic and Republican congressional leaders had endorsed the idea of health care reform in 1992 and 1993, and dozens of reform bills were introduced in Congress. Republican leaders had endorsed some key components of comprehensive reform, including universal coverage, and influential players such as Senate Minority Leader Robert Dole (R–Kans.) and moderate Republicans Bob Packwood (R–Ore.) and David Durenberger (R–Minn.) had publicly expressed a willingness to work with Clinton—although by the summer of 1994 all had backed away from their expressions of support (Skocpol 1996, 162–163). The four major bills in the House—the Clinton plan, and alternatives sponsored by James Cooper (D–Tenn.), Jim McDermott (D–Wash.), and Robert Michel (R–Ill.) together had 296 cosponsors among them. Even allowing for strategic behavior by legislators, this suggests considerable support for some sort of reform.

Early survey data show strong support for the Clinton plan, with support approaching 60 percent in some surveys taken in the aftermath of Clinton's national health care address (see Figure 3.1).[4] In the months after it was announced, however, that support fragmented to the point where more people actually _opposed_ the plan than supported it, even as they continued to approve of the idea of reform. By February 1994, as shown in Figure 3.1, support for the plan was consistently below 50 percent, and by March, opponents outnumbered supporters.

The strong initial support, however, obscures the existence of significant discrepancies in how the public viewed health care reform in general, as opposed to support for specific measures. There is substantial though not universally accepted evidence to support the contention that, although the public favored

FIGURE 3.1

Public Support for Clinton Health Plan

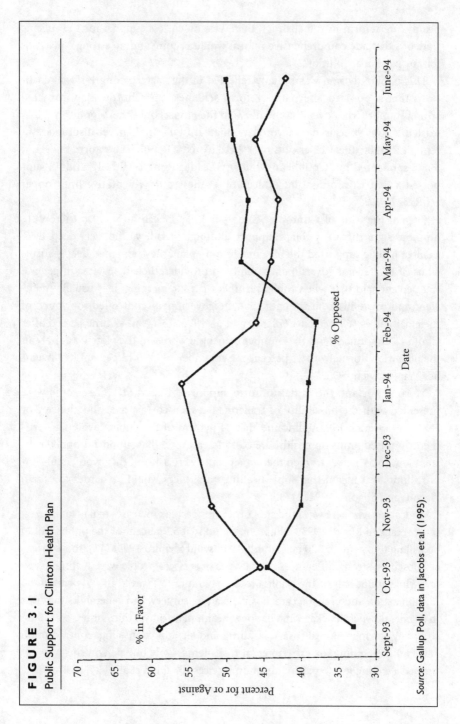

Source: Gallup Poll, data in Jacobs et al. (1995).

health care reform in the abstract, there was much less support for the specific tradeoffs that any comprehensive reform would require and no strong consensus for any particular solution.

This public division was initially reflected in the varying congressional coalitions that supported alternative reform schemes: the Clinton plan attracted strong support from over 100 members in the House, but other significant blocs existed. About 90 legislators favored a Canadian style single-payer insurance system (H.R. 1200, the McDermott bill), 141 favored a Republican reform bill (H.R. 3080, sponsored by Republican Minority Leader Robert Michel), and 48 supported a centrist proposal introduced by Tennessee Representative Jim Cooper (H.R. 3222).

Even at the time of Clinton's September 1994 speech, moreover, there were ominous signs that the public's support, although broad, was not very deep. Even as most people supported the idea of Clinton's plan, they remained deeply suspicious of the federal government's ability to provide efficient services in general (69 percent said that when the government runs something, it is usually inefficient and wasteful), and thought that the government controlled too much of their daily lives (65 percent) (Blendon et al. 1995, 13). And as time passed after Clinton's announcement, the number of people who said they knew a lot about the plan went down, from 21 percent in September 1993 to 13 percent in November (Yankelovich 1995, 15).

More important, the initial uniform support dropped off once people were presented with the possibility of tradeoffs between cost, access, and choice. For example, a March 1993 poll found that 84 percent of the public favored government-imposed limits on health care cost increases. Yet that support dropped substantially, to 51 percent, when the same people were asked if they would still support limits if it meant that some health care services would be harder to obtain (Jacobs and Shapiro 1994, 213).

And, although there was mild support for modest tax increases to pay for universal coverage (a March 1993 Gallup poll found that 52 percent of the public would be willing to pay up to $20 per month; Jacobs and Shapiro 1994, 211), this consensus obscured strong differences in the types of services people were willing to pay for: while about half of the public would pay more in taxes to include childhood immunization and prenatal care, hospitalization, surgery, and general doctor visits in a general benefit package in a national health plan, only a third or less would do so to pay for mental health services, drug and alcohol counseling, contraception and family planning, or experimental treatments. Only one person in seven expressed a willingness to pay for abortion services (Blendon et al. 1994, 1542).

Opponents of the Health Security Act embarked on a conscious strategy to undermine this initial public support by capitalizing on public fears of intrusive "big government" and the prospect, as some put it, of health care delivered with the efficiency of the Postal Service and the courtesy of the Department of Motor Vehicles. Republicans saw an opportunity to gain significant advantages for their party by adopting a no-compromise opposition strategy. As Skocpol describes it:

> By late May of 1994, during a retreat over Memorial Day weekend, Dole and other Republican congressional leaders accepted the assessment of pollsters and consultants that their party would do better electorally by refusing to compromise with the congressional Democrats. Sensing that big victories lay ahead in November 1994, congressional Republican leaders in effect accepted the Gingrich-Armey-Kristol[5] formula for all-out opposition (Skocpol 1996, 163).

With Republicans united in their opposition, and unwilling to seek common ground with Clinton and other reform-minded Democrats, significant reform had no chance.

There is more to this story, though, than simply out-of-control special interests or partisan wrangling. Joe White has pointed out that if the health care lobby was as powerful as its critics claimed, it would have been able to keep Congress from imposing regulatory constraints and stringent cost control measures on doctors and hospitals in the 1980s (White 1995, 377).

One the one hand, Congress had an opportunity to make policy of a clear collective nature (in its national policymaking role). On the other hand, legislators had to broker the multitude of interests and values at stake and pay attention to how their actions were playing at home (the local representative role). This would be difficult under the best of conditions, although it has happened. Whatever the merits of the Health Security Act, and despite successes in previous efforts to embark on large social programs (including Social Security, Medicare, Medicaid, and the like), there were bound to be *significant* disputes—both ideological and self-interested—arising over any effort to restructure nearly one-sixth of the economy, with all of the concomitant changes to existing relationships among citizens, medical professionals, insurance companies, and the dozens of other groups with a stake in the system. Yet those who question the "conventional wisdom" about the public's role in the collapse of health reform do not give enough credence to serious divisions in public opinion, which made the initial coalition favoring reform extremely unstable.

Mark Peterson, a political scientist who studies health policy issues, provides a deft description of the dilemma members faced as the debate evolved:

[The] influence of the myriad of special interests with a serious economic stake in health care reform, especially in maintaining the status quo, could be overwhelmed by the public salience of health care reform and general constituency pressure on Congress that favored substantial policy change. When the public cares about something, on the broad strokes Congress is a decidedly responsive institution and now a far more open one. When the public message is muddled, when fear of change grips the heart more than the possibilities of reform entice the mind, Congress as a collective body rarely displays a willingness to go it alone. Members of Congress began to fear supporting anything even more than they feared supporting nothing. By some accounts, many legislators were relieved that the reform effort died gracelessly at the end of the last session before they were forced to actually vote on any part of it (Peterson 1995, 426).

Thus, as public opinion turned against health care reform, many members of Congress saw themselves as acting in the public's interest, while others extracted rational individual and partisan gains from their opposition.

While the presence of a policy dilemma for Congress on the health care issue was unclear (because of the shifting collective judgment), instabilities of public opinion produced a strong institutional collective dilemma: although the public was extremely unhappy about Congress's performance on health care, that displeasure focused on the *institution*, not on individual legislators. Members acting in their own self-interest hurt the institution, but individual members emerged unscathed. Data from the National Election Study, an extensive survey conducted in each election year by a research group at the University of Michigan, make this clear. In October and November 1994, 74 percent of the public disapproved of Congress's handling of health care (see Table 3.1). Simultaneously, though, 81 percent of those surveyed *approved* of their own representative generally (this question, though, did not ask specifically about what the representative did on health care). And at least on this issue, voters' evaluation of Congress had virtually nothing to do with what they thought of the incumbent legislator.

Support for the existence of the institutional collective dilemma is very clear: individual legislators *did* make individual- and party-based rational decisions to oppose significant reform, even to overtly obstruct reform, when public support dropped, even though the result was an even greater level of public disillusionment with Congress. By October 1994, only 21 percent of the public approved of Congress, down from 33 percent in August 1993, and as we noted above, most people were extremely displeased with the way Congress handled health care. Nevertheless, voters did not punish the Republicans even though party members made no secret of their desire to block reform efforts. Nor did the electorate reward those active in pushing for reform: Harris Wofford (D–Pa.), whose 1991 Senate election served as the bellwether of pro-reform public sentiment, lost in

TABLE 3.1

Evaluations of Individual Representatives and Attitudes Toward Congress on Health Care

% of Public Approving of Congress's Handling of Health Care:	26%
% Disapproving	74%
% of Public Approving Own Representative's Job Performance	81%
% Disapproving	19%

	Opinion of Congress's Handling of Health Care	
Opinion of One's Own Representative	Approve	Disapprove
Approve	84%	80%
Disapprove	16%	20%

Source: National Election Study, 1994 Post-election survey. Interuniversity Consortium for Political and Social Research.

his bid for re-election in 1994. Tennessee Democrat Jim Cooper, sponsor of the Cooper plan, was trounced in his 1994 Senate bid, losing to Republican Fred Thompson, 60 to 39 percent.

Finally, we note that the Clinton plan was derailed long before the inevitably disruptive and controversial issue of abortion was addressed. The question, of course, was whether abortion would be a covered service under the minimum benefit package that employers would provide. The legislation as introduced was ambiguous, referring only to "services for pregnant women" (H.R. 3600, Section 1116 [1]). Congress never did settle the issue one way or the other, often making contradictory changes. In July 1994, for example, the Senate Finance Committee voted to include abortion as a benefit, at the same time that it also voted to allow employers and insurance companies to refuse to include certain benefits on the grounds of moral objections, and to permit states to maintain or expand existing restrictions on abortion services. Pro-life groups objected that these actions made abortion a federally mandated benefit, while pro-choice groups opposed the employer exemption (Rubin 1994a, 1871). That same month, Catholic leaders urged Church members to oppose any health care legislation that provided abortion services. One implication that can be drawn from this discussion is that the deeper one delved into the details of the policy, the more political land mines would be uncovered, which meant that the coalition in support of the legislation would unravel even more. This directly undermines the view that if the public had had a better understanding of the reforms they would have been more supportive. Indeed, just the opposite appears to have been the case.

Under what circumstances, then, will Congress be able to act in the collective interest? As we note above, this depends on one's definition of the collective interest. We provided strong evidence that health care reform created an institutional dilemma for Congress. Republicans were able to use public dissatisfaction with Congress to their advantage, which adds a partisan element to the individual roots of the institutional dilemma. That is, it was clearly rational for the Republicans to oppose this and other major legislation that came up in the summer of 1994 even if it meant making the institution look bad, because that opposition played a role in their winning House and Senate majorities in the 1994 midterm elections. They gambled that a collective "running for Congress by running against Congress" would undermine the majority party, and their gamble paid off. On the policy side, the dilemma is not as clear. As public support for the Clinton plan unraveled, members of Congress *were* acting, for the most part, in what they perceived to be their constituents' interests.

Our intent here is not to insist that ours are the only correct interpretations of these two cases; indeed, political scientists, pundits, and policy analysis will argue over the failure of the Health Security Act and tobacco reform for years. Instead, we mean to demonstrate that when complex legislation fails, the explanations are often complex, and it is usually wrong to attribute failure simply to the nefarious effect of "special interests." More important, placing legislation within the context of the collective dilemma analytical framework can clear the way for a better understanding of what motivates legislators when they face difficult and complex decisions.

The Changing Context of the Collective Dilemma

Thus far we have argued that the collective dilemma is an inherent characteristic of the legislative system, that Congress is no "worse" than it has ever been, and that the collective dilemma unfolds in ways that are more complex than often captured in the popular press, which likes to portray Congress as the servant of special interests. Nevertheless, Congress has changed in recent decades in ways that have further decentralized the institution and aggravated the difficulties of legislating collectively. Some of the developments are the result of past efforts at congressional reform (especially those in the 1970s, which we describe in Chapter

4), which have made Congress more open, less hierarchical, and less controllable by the leadership. Others are the consequence of broader changes in the political environment that have changed the face of politics and governing in the United States: the decline of political parties as a unifying force in government and the electorate, the escalating cost of campaigns, and the rise of television. Some are internal, especially the increasing transparency of congressional operations and the decline of norms that govern behavior, through open committee meetings, televised proceedings, and recorded electronic votes. The common theme to all of these changes is that individual legislators find it easier and more individually rational to pursue their own interests, and more difficult and less rational to focus their efforts on collective enterprises. There will, of course, be exceptions to this rule, and we are speaking of general tendencies rather than of absolute predictions. In essence, there are fewer forces pushing members together to act collectively, and more centrifugal forces pushing them apart (Loomis 1998, 13).

Before we discuss these changes in the context of the collective dilemma, we have two caveats. First, it is a mistake to characterize these recent developments as signifying a radical change in congressional organization or functioning. Our historical review of the collective dilemma shows that members have always faced, and responded to, these sorts of pressures and problems. Chapter 4 shows that Congress has always gone through cycles of centralization and decentralization, responsibility and responsiveness. Second, we do not accept the typical picture of a totally fragmented and virtually unleadable Congress. In many respects, party leadership and loyalties among members are stronger now than in the halcyon days of the 1950s and early 1960s (Rohde 1991; Rae 1998; Evans and Oleszek 1997). As we discuss in Chapter 4, the reforms of 1995 recentralized a great deal of control in the leadership.

Politician-Centered Politics

Candidates today are elected largely on the basis of their own efforts: their own organization, connections, skills, and fund-raising efforts. Parties no longer play the central role in candidate recruitment or running campaigns.[6] Alan Ehrenhalt summarizes this change in the American political landscape: "Who sent us the political leaders we have? There is a simple answer to that question. They sent themselves. And they got where they are through a combination of ambition, talent, and the willingness to devote whatever time was necessary to seek and hold office" (1991, 19).

When candidates are elected on their own, they have a base of support that is independent of parties, and therefore they tend not to feel strongly attached to the parties. This undermines party leaders' ability to build coalitions and harms the institution's collective decisionmaking capacity. Once members are in office, they do everything they can to keep their constituents happy and get reelected. As we argued in Chapter 1, this is the source of the individual-level basis for the collective dilemma.

Members have dedicated an increasing portion of congressional staff to district and state level issues and casework to attempt to secure their political base (Cain, Ferejohn, and Fiorina 1987; Mayhew 1974; Fiorina 1989). This increase in local staff fits squarely within the collective dilemma framework. Casework is valuable to legislators in the sense that there are almost no disadvantages to performing it. It creates goodwill among constituents and serves as useful advertising. At the same time, however, there are some collective costs to placing too much emphasis on constituency service. It can tarnish the reputation of Congress if the public comes to view a particular incident as inappropriate (as happened when five senators provided assistance to a central figure in the savings and loan scandal of the 1980s, Charles Keating). It can interfere with substantive legislative duties, distracting members and their staffs from their deliberative and lawmaking functions.[7]

While keeping in touch with constituents is an important activity for members of Congress, more members say they spend "a great deal of time" meeting with constituents in their district or state than almost any other activity (these data were collected in a survey that was conducted by the Joint Committee on the Organization of Congress in 1993). Of the 152 members of Congress who answered the survey, 68 percent said they spend a "great deal of time" on this activity, while another 30 percent said they spend a "moderate amount of time" meeting with constituents at home. Meeting with constituents in Washington was third on the list, consuming a "great deal" of time for 45 percent and a "moderate amount" of time for 50 percent of members (attending committee meetings was second, with 48 percent saying they spent a "great deal" of time on that activity). In contrast, only 6 percent of members said they spend a "great deal" of time working with party leaders on coalition building (U.S. Congress 1993, 275–280). Gaylord Nelson, a former senator from Wisconsin, said, "Some days I had someone in my office every 15 minutes. Seventy percent of my time, or maybe 80 percent, was spent on nonlegislative matters. Constituents judge their senators on how much crap the senator is sending them. The less legislating and the more campaigning you do the better legislator you are perceived to be" (quoted in Ehrenhalt 1991, 235).

Another implication of politician-centered politics in Congress is that members do not have any time to spend with their colleagues. The typical day for a member of Congress is twelve to fourteen hours long, packed full with committee meetings (often with three meetings scheduled at the same time), roll call votes, meetings with constituents, more committee meetings, and then a fund-raising reception in the evening. In running this rat race, there is very little time to get to know fellow members of Congress, or even talk much to them. One former senator who left in 1980, Edmund Muskie (D–Maine), said, "You don't get to see other senators very often and you rarely get a chance to discuss serious issues with them. Days go by when you don't run into more than one or two senators." Another senator, Thad Cochran (R–Miss.) complained, "There is very little socializing here. If I have any free time I spend it with my staff. You begin to feel introverted and self-centered" (quoted in Ehrenhalt 1991, 233). This insulation from each other has implications for the decline of comity in Congress that we discuss in the next section. Members who don't know each other personally are less likely to treat one another with respect, and are less likely to be able to work productively together to pass legislation.

Changes in Institutional Norms

The efficiency of the legislative process of the Congress of the 1950s and 1960s was aided by a set of formal and informal norms, including seniority, reciprocity ("you scratch my back and I'll scratch yours"), comity (treating other members with respect), institutional loyalty, specialization, and apprenticeship. The latter two norms required that new legislators be "seen and not heard," work hard on developing their expertise in a specific area, and then make their legislative mark after they learned the ropes. These norms made collective decisionmaking easier by lending order to the legislative process, valuing hard legislative work over "showboat" publicity seeking, and aiding coalition building.

The current perceived wisdom is that nearly all of these norms have either declined or disappeared since the 1970s. New members, starting with the ambitious Watergate class of 1974—which brought eighty-six freshmen to the House, many with substantial political experience—expect to have an immediate impact, and refuse to defer quietly to their senior colleagues. Burdett Loomis links this ambition to the candidate-centered politics discussed above. The 1974 class had an ambitious policy agenda, but they also knew that they had to take care of the folks back home if they wanted to stay in office. This created a new breed of entrepreneurial politician that bucked traditional norms. Tony Coelho (D–Calif.), a member of the 1974 class and consummate insider and team-player, commented that the class of 1974 "set an example for other classes by striking out as individuals and developing their own power centers. They became independent and they didn't become beholden to the leadership" (quoted in Loomis 1988, 9). Journalist William Schneider concurs: "The class of '74 was dominated by politicians whose inclinations were anti-establishment, whose careers were independent of political party, and who had to survive in unfriendly political territory" (1989, 39).

Comity, institutional loyalty, and seniority have also gone by the boards. The decline of comity and institutional loyalty clearly undermines the collective decisionmaking capacity of Congress. Eric Uslaner, in a study of collegiality in Congress, noted the deterioration in the norm of institutional patriotism or the "commitment to the chamber and its honor" (Uslaner 1993, 38). Whereas members had historically been protective of Congress's reputation, "leaders and followers alike now respond to the coalitions of the moment. The institution and its customs command far less obeisance" (1993, 38). Uslaner argues that comity is important for deliberation and compromise. You are not as likely to compromise with someone who calls you "big, fat, and out of control" as one House member called former Speaker Tip O'Neill. To Uslaner, "[d]eclining trust in other people has led to increased budget deficits, higher agricultural price supports, and fewer major laws enacted by Congress" (1993, 18).

Ideological and partisan differences were further intensified in the 1980s and 1990s. In the late 1990s, members of Congress who recognized that tensions were high attempted to rectify the situation by holding a retreat in Hershey, Pennsylvania, that was intended to help restore a level of civility to the House (it didn't work). While such efforts are a step in the right direction, it is not clear that they will be able to reverse a two-decade-long trend. To the extent that these norms have declined, the likelihood of the collective dilemma clearly increases.[8]

While it is clear that many of these norms *have* eroded, as we have noted before, historical comparisons must be made with care because of the tendency to romanticize about how great everything was in the "good 'ol days." Richard Hall, for example, provides evidence, based on an extensive analysis of participation in committee activity, that freshmen in 1961–1962 and 1981–1982 were "less seen" than their senior colleagues, but no less likely to "be heard" (1996, 165–172). He takes this as evidence that freshmen are abstaining from participating for rational reasons (related to their experience), rather than because of the admonitions of their senior colleagues, as would be held by the apprenticeship norm. Therefore, as was true with the public opinion data, there may be more consistency across historical periods on congressional norms than dramatic change. Furthermore, the Congress of the 1950s was hardly the ideal of democratic participation and representativeness. Efficient lawmaking comes at a price.

Costs of Campaigns

In 1978, an incumbent running for reelection to the House spent an average of $112,000. In 1996, this figure had increased by over 500 percent, to $679,000. Senate elections are more difficult to analyze, since not everyone runs during each cycle. But, holding the cohort constant still permits comparisons across years. In 1978, the average Senate candidate (both incumbents and challengers) spent $951,000. Eighteen years later—or three terms—in that cohort of elections the average spending was $3.6 million, an increase of almost 300 percent (Ornstein, Mann, and Malbein 1998, table 3–3).

The exploding costs of congressional campaigns have had an effect on the collective dilemma in two ways: on the time that members can devote to lawmaking and on the party's leadership tasks. The Center for Responsive Politics conducted a survey of former members of Congress, asking them about the influence of money in the political process. (Their assumption was that the retired members would be more forthcoming than those who were still serving in office.) The results of the survey, which were published in a book called *Speaking Freely*, are revealing. The study noted that "members were almost one in defining the number-one problem . . . that the system forced them to spend too much time raising money—time, they said, they wanted to devote to legislative duties. Many were expressing real, deeply felt concerns about the damage this does to the institution of Congress" (Schram 1995, 37). For example, Representative Leslie Byrne (D–Va.) said:

> You're constantly drawn by the siren song of trying to raise money for your race. And I think it's particularly true of the House, where you have to run every two years. This last race I raised $1.2 million and it was constantly, "I should be making more phone calls"—I needed to constantly raise money. [It is] a very real distraction from the real business of legislating (quoted in Schram 1995, 38).

The impact on party leadership is twofold. First, as campaign costs have increased, the party's share of the total amount of money spent has stayed flat, or has even fallen slightly (see Figures 3.2 and 3.3). In House campaigns, direct contributions from parties to candidates is a minuscule 4 to 8 percent of the total. Matters are not much better in the Senate (7 to 12 percent). This limited role for political parties reinforces the candidate-centered nature of politics described above and undermines collective decisionmaking. David Durenberger, a former senator from Minnesota, made the implications of this pattern crystal clear, "Why the hell should I care about the party? The fact of the matter is that the Minnesota Republican party has never given me a nickel in the 16 years in the United States Senate" (quoted in Schram 1995, 119).

The second impact on party leadership is the difficulties that the fund-raising process imposes on their scheduling and coalition-building duties. If members are out raising money, they cannot be on the floor voting or meeting with the leadership. Senator George Mitchell (D–Maine) explained part of this problem:

FIGURE 3.2

Sources of House Campaign Funds

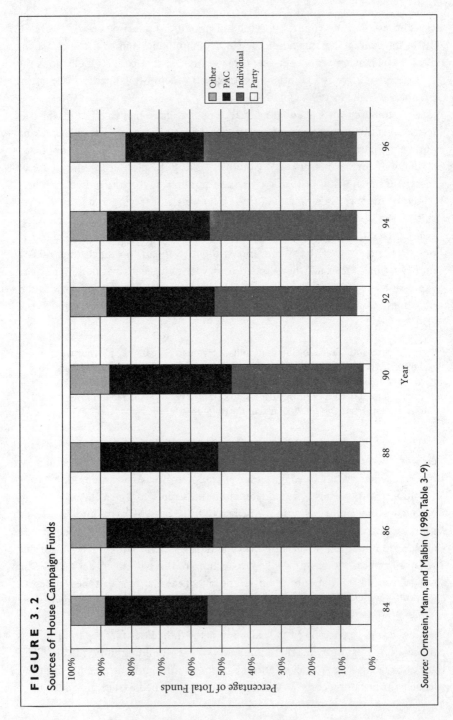

Source: Ornstein, Mann, and Malbin (1998, Table 3–9).

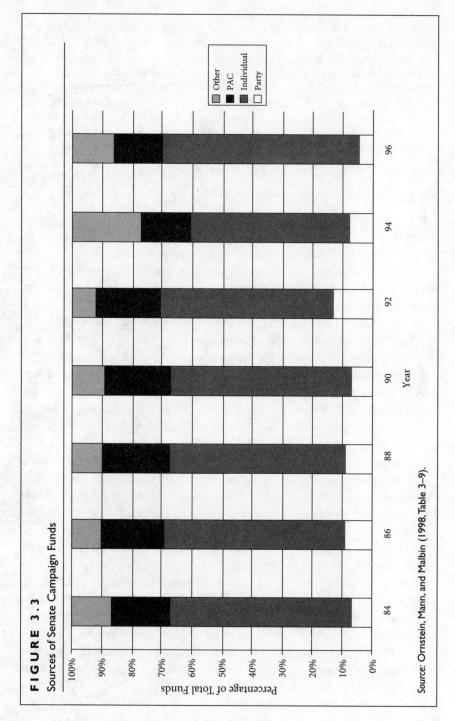

FIGURE 3.3

Sources of Senate Campaign Funds

Source: Ornstein, Mann, and Malbin (1998, Table 3–9).

As Senate Majority Leader, one of my responsibilities has been to schedule the operations of the Senate. And I can say to you that there's hardly a day in the past six years
when I've been Majority Leader when one or more senators hasn't called me and
asked me not to have a vote at a certain time. . . . One of the most common reasons is
that they are either holding or attending a fund-raising event that evening. . . . If I
put all the requests together, the Senate would never vote. I once had my staff keep a
list of such requests on one day . . . and had I honored all of the requests, there would
not have been a vote that day. It covered the period from nine a.m. until midnight
(quoted in Schram 1995, 37–38).

Technological Changes and the Mass Media

There are important changes in Congress's external environment that have
changed the mechanisms of representation and which provide both organized interests and members with new ways of mobilizing and communicating support
and opposition: the influence of direct-mail, fax, and e-mail technologies that
make it easier and less expensive to mobilize groups and, most important, the increasing importance of television in political campaigns. These tools give members a direct link to the people, something that enhances responsiveness but undermines responsibility. The rise of television ads and the thirty-second spot as
the main tool of campaigning has had serious implications for democratic accountability. Voters rarely receive enough information in a thirty-second spot to
make informed judgments on complex issues, and of course the message is always
coming from a specific perspective, so the possibility for manipulation of voters is
high (West 1997, chapter 10). Furthermore, parties are largely removed from this
process, which further undermines their influence over members.

It is important to note, however, that these developments often work at cross-
purposes. While there is no doubt that the increasing cost of campaigns has raised
the visibility and importance of large campaign contributions (which in turn
benefits concentrated interests), countervailing technologies have vastly increased
the ability of broad grassroots efforts to pressure legislators. The impact of these
cross-pressures is shown by the influence of grassroots social conservative move-
ments within the Republican party. As the party struggles with the issue of prag-
matism versus fidelity to long-cherished conservative social causes, business interests are increasingly frustrated with what they see as an inward-looking
populism on the part of Republican (G.O.P.) leaders (Neikirk 1998). Therefore,
these grassroots efforts can often serve to balance, or even counteract, the advantages the wealthy, organized interests have through campaign finance. However, as
we explore below, campaign finance is one area where the grass roots have not
taken hold and the collective dilemma looms large.

The Collective Dilemma in Action:
The Saga of Campaign Finance Reform

Few contemporary issues bring the collective dilemma into sharper relief than campaign finance reform. The 1990s regime governing campaign finance, which was established in the 1970s, has created a system that nobody likes. Persuasive evidence suggests that almost everyone—and this includes those individuals and organizations who seem to benefit the most from the current system—thinks that campaign finance requires a major overhaul. Romano Mazzoli, a Democratic House member from Kentucky, lamented, "The members would love nothing better than to get off this treadmill. The lobbyists would love nothing more that to get off this treadmill. But we're captive to the situation" (Schram 1995, 125). Modern practices have led to an overwhelming and corrosive public cynicism about both Congress as an institution and politics in general.

The 1990s campaign finance law was enacted after reports of excesses in the 1972 presidential election and was specifically designed to limit the influence that large donors have on the political process. The major elements, which are set forth in Table 3.2, are contribution limits for individuals and political action committees and the creation of a public finance system for presidential elections. The original statute also imposed spending caps on House and Senate elections, but the Supreme Court voided these as unconstitutional (in *Buckley v. Valeo*).

An individual may give no more than $1,000 to a congressional candidate for an election (the law counts primaries and general elections as separate elections, so a candidate who runs in both can accept $2,000). In addition, the total amount any person can give to all federal candidates is $25,000 every two years. Labor unions and corporations are barred from making direct contributions to candidates. The intent of these restrictions is, without dispute, to reduce the influence of large con-tributors over candidates and protect the integrity of the electoral process. But in 1996, this system broke down because of an explosion of spending not covered by contribution or spending limits. Many of the problems occurred in the presidential election, in part because of allegations that the Democratic Party and President Clinton accepted money from foreign citizens (which is illegal) and allowed the practice of having large contributors stay overnight in the White House. Democrats, in response, charged that the Republicans also raised foreign money and that the campaign finance charges were a thinly disguised effort to bring down the president.

What is not in dispute is that there was a bipartisan effort to flout the intent of the campaign finance law by raising huge sums in "soft money." Soft money (or, technically, "nonfederal account funds") is money raised and spent by political par-ties on party-building activities, generic issue education campaigns, and efforts to

TABLE 3.2
Campaign Finance Law

	Congressional Elections	Presidential Elections
Individual Contribution Limits	$1,000 per candidate per election $25,000 limit on what one person can contribute, total, to all federal candidates and parties	$1,000 per candidate (in primaries only)
National Political Party Contributions to Candidates	$20,000 per election for House candidates $17,500 total for Senate candidates plus another $10,000 per election	No contributions permitted to publicly funded candidates
Contributions by Corporations and Labor Unions	Prohibited	Prohibited
Political Action Committee Contribution Limits	$5,000 per candidate per election	Same as Congress, but no contributions permitted to publicly funded candidates
Public Funding	None	Primary: matching funds General: lump-sum grant (approximately $66 million in 1996)
Spending Limits	None	Publicly funded candidates must adhere to overall spending limit, as well as limits in each state

Source: Federal Election Commission (1996).

raise turnout. Compared to direct contributions to candidates, soft money is virtually unregulated: individuals may contribute unlimited amounts, and corporations and labor unions may also make soft money donations. In 1996, corporations and wealthy individuals made enormous contributions (over $1 million in some cases, and there were dozens of contributions over $100,000) to both the Democratic and Republican parties.[9] As candidates and parties found ways to utilize soft money in ways that directly benefited candidates—clearly violating the spirit of the soft money exception, if not the letter—levels of spending exploded. The parties raised $83 million in soft money in 1992 and $102 million in 1994, but in 1996 spending more than doubled, to $262 million. This overwhelms the $5.9 million that parties spent on direct contributions to candidates for national office in 1995–1996.

The collective dilemma is clearly in evidence here. There is virtually unanimous agreement that the campaign finance system requires some basic reforms. The public agrees. The wealthy and politically active agree. Most important, even legislators appear to agree on the need for change. It is hardly in dispute that the current system harms Congress as an institution through increasing public cynicism, distrust, and disapproval. And there is no question that the time devoted to raising funds is time that is not available for any other purpose. When Mel Levine (D–Calif.) decided to give up his House seat and run for the Senate, he was forced to raise far more than he did for any of his earlier campaigns. Levine, who was considered a competent and skilled legislator, found that the need to raise campaign funds interfered with his other duties: "[I]t just drained my time and ability to do anything else. It just crippled my ability to do my job properly in my final term" (Schram 1995, 42).

Yet reform has so far proven excruciatingly difficult, with several major efforts failing in the mid to late 1990s, and the collective dilemma framework explains why: the problem is that there are enough members of Congress for whom the *individual* stake in the system outweighs the clear *institutional and collective* pressure for reform. Even though there are significant institutional consequences, the individual incentives are such that reform is hard to achieve. Moreover, most reforms would have a disproportionate impact on one of the major parties, something which makes consensus almost impossible. To give one example, many Republicans favor laws that would make it much harder for labor unions to raise and spend money on political efforts. This effort, no doubt, is motivated by the fact that in recent elections more than 90 percent of labor politic action committee (PAC) money went to Democratic candidates. Democrats, conversely, are more enthusiastic about banning soft money contributions because Republicans raise significantly more of this type of campaign funds. What is good for the Democrats is probably not so beneficial for the Republicans, and vice versa.

In campaign finance the problem is definitely not the absence of external pressure for change. As we noted above, almost everyone agrees on the need for basic reforms. A 1997 *Los Angeles Times* poll, for example, found that 63 percent of the public thinks the campaign finance system needs either "fundamental overhaul" or "many changes." Nearly three quarters of the public (73 percent) thought that Democrats and Republicans were equally responsible for campaign finance abuses in congressional races, and 96 percent thought that Clinton had engaged in objectionable behavior to raise funds during the 1996 campaign (LAT National Poll #398, September 1997). A June 1998 poll, conducted by the Pew Research Center for the People and the Press, found that over half of the people who had been following the story closely believed that Clinton made foreign policy decisions favorable to China because of illegal campaign contributions by the Chinese government. In that same poll, 81 percent said that reforming the campaign finance system was very important or fairly important to the country.

Even large campaign contributors (defined as those who gave more than $200 to a single candidate in 1995–1996) express disappointment. A recent survey of such large contributors, who are wealthy, well-connected, and politically active, found that almost one-third say the system is "broken and needs to be replaced." An additional 45 percent say the system has problems and needs to be changed. An overwhelming majority think that legislators routinely press donors for more money (80 percent), and three-quarters favor an outright ban on soft money (Green et al. 1998).[10]

Surprisingly, most members of Congress appear to dislike the campaign finance system as well. Not only is public criticism by members increasingly common (Lieberman 1998; Schram 1995), but many legislators are more and more frustrated by the need to raise large amounts of campaign cash. "Members," concluded the author of a set of interviews with ex-members of the House and Senate, "complained that the system forced them to spend too much time raising money—time, they said, that they wanted to devote to their legislative duties. Many were expressing real, deeply felt concerns about the damage this does to the institution of Congress" (Schram 1995, 37). More systematic data confirm this anecdotal evidence. In 1993, the Joint Committee on the Organization of Congress surveyed members to gauge their opinion about how they wished to spend their time. When asked which tasks they wished to spend *more* time on, fundraising ranked dead last. The two things that members most wanted to devote additional time to were (1) studying and reading about legislation and (2) participating in or watching floor debate (U.S. Congress 1993, 281–287).

Congress's inability to enact campaign finance reform legislation stems from the imbalance in the individual versus institutional incentives that legislators face. Despite the persistent public criticism of the *institution* over campaign finance reform, voters have so far failed to express their discontent by holding individual legislators accountable. In 1998, for example, although the public was indisputably unhappy about the campaign finance system and believed that it gives too much influence to well-funded special interests, it was not an issue which voters expect congressional candidates to discuss. When voters were asked in June 1998 which issues they most wanted congressional candidates to talk about during the up-coming election season, campaign finance reform failed to register at all. As Table 3.3 shows, voters were most interested in what candidates had to say about educa-tion, taxes and spending, social security, crime, and family issues. Fewer than 1 percent of respondents mentioned campaign finance reform, putting it behind immigration, highway construction, and drugs as issues important to the voters.

Legislators who oppose campaign finance reform no doubt remember the lessons of 1990–1994, which involved partisan warfare and ultimately disappoint-ment for the reformers. Partisan differences (culminating with a presidential veto in the 102nd Congress) prevented the adoption of any bill during the Bush admin-istration. When Clinton was elected in 1992, reformers hoped that the partisan ob-stacles had been removed and thus dramatic changes in the status quo, including caps on spending coupled with public financing, could be made. However, serious campaign reform bogged down because of differences between the versions passed by the House and the Senate. The House passed a bill on November 22, 1993, by a 255 to 175 margin that included partial public financing of House elections, spending limits, and aggregate caps on PAC money and contributions of more than $200. The Senate bill, which passed on June 17, 1993, by a 62 to 37 margin, banned PACs, stripped most of the public financing provisions, and implemented

---

TABLE 3.3

What One Issue Would You Most Like to Hear the Candidates in Your State or District Talk About? (Respondents Could Name Up to Three Issues)

Education	20%
Taxation	12%
Crime/Violence	12%
Jobs/Economy	11%
Social Security	8%
Health Care	5%
Campaign Finance	<1%

Source: Pew Research Center for the People and the Press, June 15, 1998.

a tax on campaigns that do not comply with spending limits. The major points of contention between the two chambers were public financing and the PAC ban. Democratic leaders spent the better part of a year ironing out the differences via informal negotiations. In September 1994, however, after an agreement had been reached, a Republican-led filibuster in the Senate prevented the appointment of a formal conference that would resolve the differences between the House and Senate versions. "I make no apologies for killing this turkey of a bill," announced Senator Mitch McConnell (R–Ky.) (Donovan 1994, 2758). Less than two months later, the Republicans swept to power in the 1994 midterm elections.

Two other attempts at campaign finance reform, in 1997 and 1998, died by filibuster as well. In January 1998, House members Christopher Shays (R–Conn.) and Marty Meehan (D–Mass.) introduced a bipartisan proposal that picked up rapid support among rank-and-file representatives. Republican party leaders, however, opposed the bill. In March 1998, Speaker Gingrich at first refused to allow the bill to come to the floor for a vote and then brought the bill to the floor under suspension of the rules, which meant it would have to obtain two-thirds approval to pass. Faced with a rising rebellion from both Republicans and Democrats, and momentum toward using a discharge petition to force the bill to the floor, Gingrich relented and agreed to schedule debate (Katz 1998, 1057).[11]

But when the bill came to the floor it was clear that the leadership had not abandoned its opposition. The rule governing debate on campaign finance legislation was unusually open, allowing for consideration of more than 250 separate amendments, including at least 11 "amendments in the nature of a substitute," each of which would replace the entire bill. The leadership's obvious strategy was to kill the bill by amending and talking it to death. Even so, the bill *did* pass the House in August 1998 (by a 252 to 179 margin, with 61 Republicans defecting from the party), surviving all of the killer amendments and harsh rules that stipulated that of the alternatives, Shays-Meehan would pass only if it was the one obtaining the most votes (under a version of a "King of the Hill" rule).

Supporters of reform hoped that House passage would force the Senate to approve the version before it (called McCain-Feingold, after its two sponsors, Senator John McCain [R–Ariz.] and Russ Feingold [D–Wisc.]). They were wrong. Opponents in the Senate filibustered the bill, and when an attempt to invoke cloture failed on a 52 to 48 vote on September 10, 1998—eight short of the 60 votes needed to end debate—the bill was declared dead. Despite public pressure and no lack of reform-minded members, campaign finance reform succumbed to the same institutional and policy dilemmas—namely the difficulty in overcoming individual incentives in order to achieve a collective policy, and a seeming inability to protect Congress's institutional prestige—that have so often afflicted Congress.

4

The Collective Dilemma and Congressional Reform

If John Calhoun, Henry Clay, or Thomas Reed, three legislative giants of the nineteenth century, were to visit the Congress at the end of the twentieth century, they would feel right at home. The legislative process, rooted in the committee system, floor deliberation, and interbranch interactions, within an arcane set of legislative rules and procedures, has the same basic look that it did 150 years ago. The visitors from the nineteenth century might wonder about the C-SPAN cameras, electronic voting, or why women are on the floor of the chamber, but one could argue that the U.S. Congress has undergone less fundamental change than any American institution in the past century other than, perhaps, baseball or apple pie (even baseball has changed, with the designated hitter, free agency, interleague play, and domed stadiums).

Despite this basic continuity, Congress is perpetually evolving. At the beginning of each Congress, the House and Senate adopt the rules that set procedures for that session. Most changes in the rules are evolutionary and incremental, but in some cases they are substantial, as in 1995 when the House abolished proxy voting in committees, eliminated legislative support organizations, slashed committee staff by a third, set term limits for the Speaker and committee chairs, and got rid of three standing committees. Non-incremental change is often preceded by a comprehensive, critical self-review of Congress's internal organization, rules and procedures, and external relations (as in 1946, 1966, and 1992). In other cases, such as the 1910 revolt against House Speaker Joe Cannon, change is precipitated by a more specific set of events within the broader context of general concerns, such as minority party rights. Finally, substantial change may occur in Congress through a series of small incremental shifts, such as the transition from the use of select committees and the Committee of the Whole to standing committees as the primary lawmaking institutions in the early nineteenth century. In this chapter we examine instances of non-incremental reforms in Congress.

The context of congressional reform is strikingly similar across each specific reform period. In each instance members of Congress expressed frustration with institutional inefficiency, workload, and "quality of life" issues, and responded to criticisms that Congress was not properly doing its job. One member testified before a joint committee on Congressional reorganization in the early 1990s:

There is virtually unanimous agreement that American people today are tired of gridlock and politics as usual. So, too, are many of us in the Congress. The Congress must become more efficient and responsive to the needs of our nation. Over the past several decades our founding fathers' vision for our government has become so bogged down in checks and balances that it is almost impossible to get anything done" (Senate Hearing 103–128 1993, 257, Representative Paul Kanjorski).

The final report from the joint committee noted: "Members were increasingly frustrated with the process; many of the large number who retired in 1992 cited their frustration as a contributing factor. And the public's usual skeptical attitude toward Congress plunged toward cynicism and major discontent as reflected in public disapproval ratings, which hit an all-time high of 77 percent in the summer of 1992" (U.S. Congress 1993, 1).

Compare those comments to the observations of the 1966 Joint Committee on the Organization of Congress: "[I]t is becoming more and more difficult for any collective decision-making entity like Congress to meet its responsibilities. . . . Many contend that Congress no longer is capable of exercising initiative in the solution of modern problems. A fundamental reason for this loss of initiative is the lack of organizational effectiveness" (Senate Report 1414 1966, 1). Or consider the APSA Committee on Congress's assessment in 1942, which served as the basis for the Legislative Reform Act of 1946: "It has always been difficult for a member of Congress to take an overall view of the interests of the country as a whole. The interests of his district or section are likely to be paramount with him, for he depends upon their support for reelection. Correspondence and specific personal services to constituents consume a large part of every member's time, leaving little for the study of important legislation" (APSA 1942, 1095). In 1910, public outrage over the autocratic leadership of Speaker Cannon was probably stronger than in any of the recent periods of Congressional reform, but the underlying concerns were basically the same as the episodes in the late twentieth century.

The more things change, the more they stay the same. Efficiency, responsiveness, and collective decisionmaking are perpetual concerns in any legislative body. This continuity, we argue, is because of the collective dilemma that lies at the heart of congressional politics and has been evident since the very first Congresses. There is a clear tension between lawmaking activity (such as the "study of important legislation") and serving district needs. There are also tradeoffs between the various goals of reformers: to the extent that an institution is more efficient and responsive, it may be less deliberative and responsible. An institution that can "get things done" and centralizes authority may not be as democratic as one that is more decentralized and responsive to each member's district needs.

Therefore, if Congress enacts reforms that will make it more responsive and democratic, it may be exacerbating the collective dilemma by reducing its lawmaking capacity and accomplishing the collective goals that would enhance its stature in the public's eyes (see Rieselbach 1994, chapter 1, for a similar argument).

If the collective dilemma is such an inherent characteristic of the legislative process, it may seem futile to talk about reforms aimed at eliminating the dilemma. Indeed, one definition of a dilemma is, "A predicament that seemingly defies a satisfactory solution" (*American Heritage Dictionary*). We agree that the collective dilemma cannot be eliminated, nor should it be. The battles between national and district interests are rooted in our Constitution. To get rid of the collective dilemma one would have to abandon our system of geographic representation. However, it is possible to reform the institution so that Congress can overcome the collective dilemma when there is a strong public consensus behind a given policy proposal.

In this chapter, we first discuss the context of congressional reform: What are the goals the members are trying to achieve through reform? How do these goals relate to alternative conceptions of representative democracy? Next we examine previous efforts at congressional reform, with special attention given to the "Republican Revolution" in 1995 and the extent to which these reforms address the collective dilemma. We also address and critique the major reforms still on the table at the end of the 1990s: measures aimed at enhancing descriptive representation (increasing the number of women and minorities in Congress), limiting the number of terms incumbents could serve, a constitutional amendment requiring a balanced budget, and the line item veto. We criticize these reforms, and one that was implemented in Congress in 1995—substantial cuts in committee staff—because they do nothing to address the collective dilemma. We argue that the reforms are based on a simplistic notion of how Congress operates, and that there is no empirical evidence to suggest that they would have the intended effect. What the reforms would do is eviscerate Congress's power and lead to an era of executive branch and interest group dominance over the policy process. Having criticized the menu of reforms, we present our own recommendations in Chapter 5.

The Goals and Trade-offs of Congressional Reform

Throughout this book we have argued that the collective dilemma imposes constraints on congressional reform. The same forces that produce collectively irrational outcomes from individually rational behavior dictate that there are certain tradeoffs inherent in the process of Congressional reform. As shown in Figure 4.1,

· ·

FIGURE 4.1

Classification of Congressional Reform

A. Reforms That Tend to Enhance the Ability to Make Collective Decisions

Strengthening party discipline in Congress
Enhancing the power of the Speaker
Secrecy in deliberations (committee voting, legislative markup)
Decreasing the minority's power to obstruct or amend legislation
Decreasing the power of committee chairs

B. Reforms That Tend to Decrease the Ability to Make Collective Decisions

Increasing the autonomy of individual legislators
Making Congress more responsive to public opinion
Decreasing the power of party leaders
Increased minority party rights (of amendment, filibustering, and so forth)
Decreasing the commitment members have to the institution

reforms that decrease the likelihood of the collective dilemma (for example, by enhancing the power of the leadership and making the institution more responsible, centralized, and insulated) also tend to make the institution less responsive, less decentralized, and less open.

However, these categories are not mutually exclusive. While a specific set of reforms would tend to favor one-half of the pair or the other, Congress will tend to exhibit *all* of the characteristics we outline to varying degrees. Congress will never be completely responsible and unresponsive, or vice versa; members of Congress will act in accordance with a trustee model of representation on some issues and the delegate model on others; and the institution is always balancing the twin goals of majority rule and minority rights. In some instances, the same reform can cut different ways. The practice of multiple referral, whereby bills were sent to more than one committee at the same time (joint referral), split up and sent to different committees (split referral), or sent to one committee and then another (sequential referral), served both individual and institutional interests (Collie and Cooper 1989, 226). (Joint referrals were abolished in 1995.) Committee members liked multiple referral because it pretty much guaranteed them a piece of the action. The leadership liked multiple referrals as well, because they could strategically divide up bills, send them to committees that were sympathetic to the leadership's policy agenda, and strike bargains across committees that would be enforced through restrictive rules (Collie and Cooper 1989, 265–266).

We also note that reforms often have unintended consequences. The "sunshine reforms" of the 1970s that opened up the legislative process to provide more accountability actually made Congress more responsive to organized interests than to the general public (Bessette 1994, 224). The practice of multiple referral contributed more to the collective dilemma than originally anticipated. For example, one reason that Clinton's health care plan did not pass in the 103rd Congress was that nine committees were involved with shaping the legislation.

As Table 4.1 shows, the same reform can have both positive and negative effects, depending on how one sees the problem. Strict majority control can speed up the legislative process, but also can trample on minority views. Allowing for extensive discussion and amendment through open rules can enhance minority representation, but it also can stall the legislative process. Reducing staff can enhance leadership power by removing alternate sources of expertise and information, but it can also reduce congressional expertise and thus create undue reliance on interest groups and the executive branch. Reform, as we noted in the title of this section, is often a trade-off between competing values and objectives.

Responsibility Versus Responsiveness

Most significant congressional reforms, we argue, must confront the tension between responsibility (which involves central lawmaking capabilities) and responsiveness (or the degree to which members try to reflect public opinion). As noted above, all institutions will have elements of both: A responsible legislature is one that focuses on problem solving, speed, and efficiency, in short, collective decisionmaking. A responsive legislature is more concerned with process than output, and above all, wants to satisfy its constituents (Rieselbach 1994, 18–19).

We reiterate that it is not possible to have it all. Reforms that tend to enhance responsibility—and thus decrease the likelihood of the collective dilemma—also tend to make the institution *less* responsive to public opinion. In contrast, reforms designed to make the institution more accountable to public opinion—and thus enhance responsiveness—also tend to increase the chances of the collective dilemma.

For example, in the 1990s, most of the pressure for reform came from the public. Reforms that are driven by this sort of widespread public disgust for Congress are, ultimately, unlikely to tackle the core problems. The public perceives that Congress is "out of touch," when in fact Congress is probably *too* responsive to constituents' needs. In a climate of public mistrust, each surviving incumbent and

TABLE 4.1

Impact of Congressional Reforms

Reform	Positive Effect	Negative Effect
Maintaining Strict Majority Control	Increases efficiency	Decreases representation of minority viewpoint
Increasing Descriptive Representation	Enhances equal representation; produces diverse legislature	To the extent that groups disagree, makes collective decisionmaking more difficult
Reducing Staff	Can enhance power of leadership, reduce individual autonomy	Increases reliance on executive branch and interest groups
Weakening Power of Party Leaders and Committee Chairs	Broadens participation, reduces likelihood of "entrenched" elite power	Decreases efficiency and difficulty of achieving collective decisionmaking
Increasing Importance of Floor Deliberation	Provides more opportunities for discussion and public education	Slows legislative process
Increasing Openness and Publicity	Results in more accountability, more opportunity for public communication	Results in grandstanding, excessive concern with public opinion
Maintaining Secrecy	Provides more opportunity for collective decisionmaking	Provides less public accountability
Establishing More Open Rules (House)	Increases opportunity for minority to participate in debate and amendment process	Results in more delay

newly elected member will try to make sure that he or she can carve out a piece of safe congressional turf, rather than trying to enhance collective responsibility.

To a large extent, in 1995 members of Congress resisted the impulse to address only issues of responsiveness. When the new Republican majority imposed some reforms in 1995, most of them were either harmless (such as getting rid of the free buckets of ice that were distributed to each member's office twice a day, a throwback to the pre-refrigerator era, or privatizing the House barber shop), or actually did some good (such as making Congress follow the private sector workplace laws, making the *Congressional Record* and other House documents available online, and including all committee votes in committee reports). Some reforms aimed at responsiveness, however, undermined responsibility. For example, proxy voting (the practice whereby the committee leaders were able to cast votes for committee members from their party who were absent) gave a substantial advantage to the majority party, and thus was an important tool for collective decisionmaking. However, the Republican Congress abolished this practice in 1995. Similarly, they cut committee staff and opened up more committee meetings to television, which reduced the policymaking abilities of the institution. However, other 1995 reforms, which we discuss in more detail below, enhanced the collective decisionmaking ability of the institution.

Majority Rule and Minority Rights

A central problem for representative democracy is to provide a voice for minority interests in a system that is dominated by the votes of the majority. The legitimacy and stability of any democracy depend, in part, on its ability to accomplish that difficult aim. The Framers' institutional solution of the separation of powers within and across levels of government provided multiple points of access for various interests and some assurance that no single interest would dominate government for extended periods. Hailed by generations of pluralists within political science, this competitive political process was thought to produce optimal results.[1] Majority tyranny was prevented by a pluralist politics in which "minorities rule," to use Robert Dahl's famous phrase (Dahl 1956, 124–151). However, for at least forty years, scholars and politicians have recognized that the system did not provide adequate representation for certain groups in society, especially racial minorities, poor people, and others who did not have organized interests to speak on their behalf.

In the context of congressional politics, battles have been waged since early in the nineteenth century to recast the balance between the right of the majority party to govern and the right of the minority to participate in the process. Early discussions of minority rights in Congress had a completely different starting point than today's focus on racial minorities or providing a voice for dissent. Rather, early nineteenth-century proponents of minority rights were interested in protecting property rights and positions of privilege. John Calhoun's famous theory of concurrent minorities held that any state could call a convention to nullify a national law that it saw as counter to its interests. This argument was applied to the principle of unlimited debate in the Senate (which had previously been established in 1806) and became the theoretical basis for the states' rights argument in defense of slavery.

As strong parties emerged in Congress in the mid-nineteenth century, the minority party developed tactics to counter the majority party. The most important of these was the "disappearing quorum," which was used between 1832 and 1890. This tactic involved refusing to be counted as present during a quorum call, which prevented the House from doing its business (under House rules, a majority of members had to be present in order to conduct business). In 1847, the minority party also secured the right to have five minutes to present and debate an amendment to a bill (a right that still exists in current House rules).

Other protections, which are described below, were added for the minority party over the years in the House and the Senate. One general point is noteworthy: The House is governed by majoritarian principles and the Senate has much stronger protections for minority rights. If a majority of the House wants to get something done, it is typically able to impose its will, through mechanisms such as the discharge petition (which allows a majority of members to force a committee to send a bill to the floor), committee assignments, and the designation of conferees (the members who serve on the committee that resolves differences between the House and Senate versions of a bill) (Krehbiel 1991, 16–19). This majoritarian principle was expressed by one of the strongest speakers in history, Joseph Cannon: "Results cannot be had except by a majority, and in the House of Representatives a majority, being responsible, should have full power and should exercise that power" (*Congressional Record*, March 19, 1910, 3436, quoted in Jones 1995, 268).

In the Senate, the minority party has a powerful tool in the filibuster (unlimited debate), which allows forty-one members to stop any piece of legislation (sixty senators are needed to stop a filibuster). Individual senators even have a great deal of power through the use of informal "holds" that can keep legislation from reaching the floor (Binder and Smith 1997, 11–12). These obstructionist tactics often lead to battles in which the majority is prevented from exerting its will. After one such fight a disgruntled senator complained, "If this is the world's greatest deliberative body . . . I'd hate to see the world's worst" (quoted in Binder and Smith 1997, 13). Despite the stronger protections of minority rights in the Senate, partisanship has been more acrimonious in the House than the Senate in the past decade (Mann and Ornstein 1992, 54–55).

The link between the tension between majority rule and minority rights and the collective dilemma is clear: If the majority party has the ability to impose its agenda, it is far less likely that the collective dilemma will emerge. If the legislature is characterized by strong minority party rights, it is more likely that narrow interests (whether they are party or policy based) will prevent the majority from having its way.

Centralization/Strong Parties Versus Decentralization/Weak Parties

The discussion of majority rule and minority rights is strongly connected to the tradeoffs between strong majoritarianism and representation of minority views. Strong parties attempt to exploit the majoritarian characteristics of Congress and the strongest parties have not had much tolerance for minority rights. Speaker Thomas Reed once remarked, "The right of the minority is to draw its salaries and its function is to make a quorum" (Fuller 1909 in Keefe and Ogul 1997, 232). Strong parties are also associated with centralization of power within the leadership. At the peak of the Speaker's power, under the leadership of Reed and Cannon, he had the power to make all appointments to committees (including control of the important Rules Committee), the power of recognition on the floor, and control over the legislative process. While today's Speaker does not have these extensive powers, the office was considerably strengthened in 1995. The Speaker's influence was expanded over committee assignments, the office maintained de facto control over the appointment of committee chairs, and House administration offices were placed under the Speaker's control. Most important, the Speaker was able to reduce the power of rivals: committee chairs (through a six-year term limit) and the legislative support organizations such as the Congressional Black Caucus and the Democratic Study Group that were important institutional bases of power for liberal causes (starting in 1995, LSOs could no longer be supported with office funds) (Evans and Oleszek 1997, 86–91). Robert Walker (R–Pa.) noted that the most important implication of limiting the committee chairs' terms was that, "Members will have to think more broadly, instead of simply rising and carving their legislative niche" (Evans and Oleszek 1997, 89). This clearly links the notion of centralization and strong parties to the diminished likelihood of the collective dilemma. If members are forced to "think more broadly," rather than fighting for their piece of legislative turf, collective decisionmaking is enhanced.

It is possible for strong leaders to exist in a period of decentralization and weak parties, as did Henry Clay in the 1810s and 1820s and Sam Rayburn in the 1940s and 1950s. Henry Clay exerted such power over his party during the presidency of John Tyler that his opponents called him "The Dictator." Clay and Rayburn were able to help the institution overcome the collective dilemma through the power of

Henry Clay. Courtesy of the Library of Congress.

their personalities, despite the locus of power residing at the committee or sub-committee level, but such examples are the exception rather than the rule.

While strong, centralized parties lessen the likelihood of the collective dilemma they do not ensure that the institutional and policy dilemmas can be overcome. The institutional dilemma will be less likely for two reasons. First, the problem of institutional maintenance is solved: the Speaker exerts iron-fisted control and his lieutenants carry out his policies. Members may still be tempted to run for Congress by running against Congress, but this is less likely if they are part of a "party team." Second, the policy dilemma is less likely because the party will articulate a clear set of policies that it will attempt to enact. However, this does not mean that the "collective good" will necessarily prevail. It is possible, as happened in the battles in the late nineteenth century over the tariff, that strong parties will simply impose one set of sectional preferences over another.

Secrecy Versus Openness

One of the hard-earned lessons of congressional reform is that well-intentioned changes often have unintended consequences. For example, the "sunshine reforms" of the 1970s, which opened up the legislative process to outside scrutiny and provided for more recorded votes in committee and on the floor, were intended to make members of Congress more accountable. The reforms, which were supported by Common Cause and other "good government" groups, certainly provided a greater degree of accountability, but they also enhanced the power of the special interests, which is exactly the opposite of the intended effect (Arnold 1990, 275). The conventional wisdom held that if legislating occurs "behind closed doors" in "smoke-filled rooms," members will cut secret deals with special interests. However, experience demonstrated that when Congress wanted to enact policies that were in the public's interest, and opposed by the special interests, ironically that is when they most needed to formulate legislation behind closed doors (as with the 1986 Tax Reform discussed in Chapter 5). Accounts of lobbyists sitting in on committee markup sessions, even actually writing the legislation, demonstrate the perverse impact of the sunshine laws at their extreme. Joseph Bessette summarizes this argument:

> [I]f we begin not with the democratic premise that the people have a right to monitor every official act of their representatives or with its cynical variant that legislators are not to be trusted, but rather with the view that most lawmakers who serve in Congress genuinely desire to promote the public good, then the question becomes whether the glare of public scrutiny and formal accountability for every vote in committee and most votes on the floor contributes to or hinders deliberation in service of

the public good. Indeed, we can identify in principle a variety of ways in which maximizing accountability and publicity can harm deliberation or, conversely, ways in which insulating legislators to some degree from public scrutiny can support and enhance deliberation in Congress (Bessette 1994, 223).

Bessette argues that an open legislative process rewards "showboating" over serious legislative work. He also notes, though he does not use our term, that the sunshine laws increase the probability that the policy dilemma will emerge. He says that greater publicity makes members more accountable to their geographic constituencies and "may make it more difficult for these putatively 'national' legislators to reason together and work toward policies in the broad national interest" (Bessette 1994, 224).

Linking Reform to Theories of Representation

The goals of reform that are adopted in any given historical period depend, in part, on the view of representation favored by congressional leaders. To what extent is it important to have descriptive representation, that is, a Congress that "looks like us?" Until recently, this form of representation did not play a prominent role in debates over congressional reform. However attention shifted to this form of representation with the creation of twenty-five new majority-minority districts (that is, congressional districts in which a majority of the constituents are a racial minority) and the "Year of the Woman" in 1992, in which record numbers of women were elected to Congress. There are various steps that Congress can take to encourage descriptive representation. First, Congress can pass legislation that encourages the creation of more majority-minority districts, as they did in the 1982 Voting Rights Act Amendments. Second, the party committees can actively recruit women and minorities to run for House and Senate seats, especially in hotly contested open-seat races (when an incumbent is not running).

The version of substantive representation that one sees as central will also shape the reform agenda. Those who favor a trustee model of representation will advocate a centralized, responsible legislative process. Those who see the delegate model as the proper representational relationship between the politician and the constituent will favor a decentralized, responsive process. We briefly discuss the range of arguments concerning these various models of representation below.

Descriptive Representation

Descriptive representation is rooted in the politician's side of the representative relationship.[2] Does the member of Congress "look like" the constituent? Is the member black or white, male or female, Catholic or Protestant? There are three positions on the value of descriptive representation. The first argues that there is a distinct value in having role models and notes the benefits that come from the simple act of being represented by someone who shares something as fundamental as skin color. One local black politician from South Carolina, Tom McCain, noted, "There's an inherent value in office holding that goes far beyond picking up the garbage. A race of people who are excluded from public office will always be second class citizens" (quoted in Davidson and Grofman 1994, 16). The intangibles of descriptive representation and the role models that help create greater trust in the system are important. Abigail Thernstrom, a critic of special policies aimed at providing descriptive representation, acknowledges the advantages of having racially diverse political bodies:

> Whether on a city council, on a county commission, or in the state legislature, blacks inhibit the expression of prejudice, act as spokesmen for black interests, dispense patronage, and often facilitate the discussion of topics (such as black crime) that whites are reluctant to raise. That is, governing bodies function differently when they are racially mixed, particularly where blacks are new to politics and where racially insensitive language and discrimination in the provision of services are long-established political habits (1987, 239).

Even if one could be assured that substantive representation was not affected by race or gender, it would not be fair if the nation were represented by 535 white males in Congress. Barney Frank (D–Mass.) argues that descriptively diverse representation is better representation:

> What we are saying is a representative assembly in which no one has lived the life of an African American in the South, in which no one has lived the life of a Hispanic in the United States, in which, let me add, there has been no gay person, or there haven't been any Jews, or there have been very, very few women, will not do as good a job of representing the country. That doesn't mean you automatically reproduce it, but that's the value that you are losing (House of Representatives 1994, 74–75).

This same logic has produced a strong commitment to racial diversity in corporate America, in higher education, and in the public sector.

The second and third positions argue that descriptive representation by itself is not useful unless it is linked to substantive representation. The left-of-center perspective argues having "black faces in high places" may come at too high a price. Robert C. Smith says, "Like the transformation of black music, it will be a hollow victory if in order to achieve equitable descriptive-symbolic representation blacks are required to sacrifice their substantive policy agendas. The new black politician would then be a shell of himself, more like a Prince or Michael Jackson than a B.B. King or Bobby Bland" (Smith 1990, 161). The right-of-center perspective recognizes the value of descriptive representation in some limited contexts, but points out that whites can adequately represent black interests and that descriptive representation often comes at a price, such as contributing to racial polarization.

Descriptive representation is important for our purposes because it is one way in which responsiveness to constituencies is measured. As noted above, the most aggressive policy aimed at providing more minority representation in the U.S. House was the creation of fifteen black-majority and ten Hispanic-majority districts in 1992. These districts were drawn by state legislatures in response to the 1982 Voting Rights Act Amendments and subsequent interpretations by the Supreme Court that mandated that minority-majority districts be drawn to permit minority populations to elect "candidates of their choice" when they were sufficiently cohesive and geographically compact (Davidson and Grofman 1994; Canon forthcoming, chapter 2). However, in a series of court cases, starting with the landmark ruling *Shaw v. Reno* (1993), the Supreme Court ruled that race could not be the predominant factor in drawing House district lines.

Most scholars and political observers concur that policies aimed at enhancing descriptive representation would actually increase the likelihood of the collective dilemma. In the majority opinion in *Shaw v. Reno,* Sandra Day O'Connor states that, "[w]hen a district obviously is created solely to effectuate the perceived common interests of one racial group, elected officials are more likely to believe that their primary obligation is to represent only the members of that group, rather than their constituency as a whole" (509 U.S. 630, 648 [1993]). This line of reasoning leads to the inescapable conclusion that white voters will not be adequately represented in black-majority districts and that black-majority districts will be yet another polarizing and decentralizing force in Congress. If black representatives are primarily looking out for black interests, or Latino representatives for Latino interests, it will be difficult to include them in the collective decision-making process.

However, research just completed by one of us demonstrates that many of the African American politicians who were elected in the new black-majority districts actually built biracial coalitions to get elected and searched for common interests that link the races rather than divide them (Canon forthcoming, chapters 3 and 4). Furthermore, even those who *campaign* by appealing only to black voters do, in fact, spend a substantial proportion of their time in Congress representing the interests of white and black voters alike. In the context of the collective dilemma, this demonstrates that policies that produce better descriptive representation also are likely to decrease the likelihood of the collective dilemma as a greater proportion of members work to enact legislation across a common set of interests.

Trustee and Delegate Models of Representation

While descriptive representation is important, it only goes so far. As A. Phillips Griffiths pointed out, we do not expect lunatics to be represented by crazy people. "While we might wish to complain that there are not enough representative members of the working class among Parliamentary representatives" he says, "we would not want to complain that the large class of stupid or maleficent people have too few representatives in Parliament; quite the contrary" (quoted in Phillips 1995, 39).[3]

Substantive representation moves beyond appearances to specify *how* the member serves the interest of the constituents. As noted in Chapter 1, two models go back at least to the time of Edmund Burke: (1) the trustee who represents the interests of constituents from a distance, weighing a variety of national, collective, local, and moral concerns; and (2) the delegate who has a simple mandate to carry out the direct desires of the voters. To the extent that members see themselves as trustees, the collective dilemma would be less likely to arise; conversely, the more delegates there are, the more likely the collective dilemma. Trustees are freed from the re-electoral pressures that produce the dilemma, while delegates constantly have their moistened fingers in the air to determine which way the electoral winds are blowing.

Hannah Pitkin advanced this discussion by noting that both of these perspectives are right and that true representation must combine both approaches. Her definition, offered more than thirty years ago, serves as the basis for much empirical research on representation today:

Representation here means acting in the interest of the represented, in a manner responsive to them. The representative must act independently; his action must involve discretion and judgment; he must be the one who acts. . . . And, despite the resulting potential for conflict between representative and represented about what is to be done, that conflict must not normally take place. The representative must act in such a way that there is not conflict, or if it occurs an explanation is called for (Pitkin 1967, 209–210, quoted in Jewell 1983, 304).

The importance of Pitkin's insight for our purposes is that congressional reforms do not have to be a series of either/or propositions. *Reforms will only tilt the
central tendencies of Congress in one direction or the other.* A centralized Congress
that is relatively insulated from outside forces would make it easier for a member
of Congress to be a trustee, while a decentralized, open institution is more consistent with the delegate model of representation. However, there will be plenty of
exceptions to these general patterns.

Previous Episodes of Congressional Reform

The history of congressional reforms demonstrates the oscillation between the
various types of reform and the tradeoffs among the various goals of reform.
Table 4.2 outlines the major episodes of congressional reform. The early nineteenth century was a period of continuous and incremental "reform." There were
no self-conscious, comprehensive examinations of legislative procedures and
structures that characterize the reforms of the twentieth century. Instead, change
came about gradually, and one could argue, without a clear plan or strategy. There
were several specific rules changes that were adopted to protect minority rights,
such as the two-thirds vote that is required to suspend the rules (1822), the five-
minute rule on amendments (1847), unlimited debate in the Senate (1806), and
the right to appeal decisions made by the chair (1828) (Binder 1995, 1403–1405),
and others that limited minority rights, such as placing limits on the number of
quorum calls (1860) (Binder 1996, 19). However, none of these reforms was comprehensive. The most far-reaching change in the early nineteenth century was the
shift from select committees to standing committees as the primary locus of legislative activity. This shift was gradual over the period of several decades, but
there is some evidence that it reflected the conscious choices of an ambitious
Speaker, Henry Clay, to centralize his power (Gamm and Shepsle 1989).

The reforms of the 1890s provide the best example of an explicit effort to reduce the likelihood of the collective dilemma. Sectional and partisan battles over
the tariff literally brought the legislative process to a standstill through the 1880s.
Dilatory motions, such as motions to adjourn or repeated quorum calls, were
used by the minority party to prevent legislation that they opposed from being
passed. The most infamous obstructionist tactic was the "disappearing quorum,"
whereby members of the minority party would refuse to allow themselves to be
counted, thus denying the chamber the 165-person quorum that was required to
do business. Speaker Thomas Reed unilaterally ended the disappearing quorum
by simply recognizing those members who were present, whether or not they
wanted to be counted. The critical juncture of the battle, which went on for three

TABLE 4.2

Major Reforms of the U.S. Congress

Year	Major Elements
1811–1825	Establishment of standing committees.
1890	Adopted Reed's Rules: expedited business by eliminating the "disappearing quorum," restricted dilatory motions, reduced a quorum in the Committee of the Whole to 100 members, established a "morning hour" calendar to facilitate consideration of important legislation.
1910–1911	Revolt against Speaker Joseph Cannon; stripped the Speaker of his chairmanship of the Rules Committee and his power to make committee assignments. After a ten-year period in which the party caucus dominated, the era of strong committees was ushered in.
1946	Legislative Reorganization Act of 1946. Restructured the committee system, dramatically cutting the number of committees; created a comprehensive budget process; required registration of lobbyists; established expectations for greater oversight of the executive branch; and enhanced the information resources of Congress.
1970–1977	Legislative Reorganization Act of 1970 (based largely on the actions of the 1965 Joint Committee on the Organization of Congress), Budget Impoundment Control Act of 1974, various rules changes imposed by the Democratic Caucus 1971–1974, and the Obey Commission 1977. This massive set of reforms decentralized the legislative process through the "subcommittee bill of rights," granted more power to the Speaker, established new budget committees and a new budget process, passed "sunshine" laws to open up the legislative process, recorded more votes in committees and on the floor, and passed a financial ethics package.
1991–1996	Congress tried to solve its image problem by eliminating some perks and establishing the Joint Committee on the Organization of Congress (1992). Republicans enacted major reforms in 1995.

days, is recounted in Figure 4.2. Equally significant were the rules changes that were adopted in February 1890 to expedite the legislative process. The organizing principles of these reforms were based on the majoritarian principle, responsibility, and the centralization of the legislative function in strong parties. Reed succinctly summarized his focus on responsibility and collective decisionmaking:

FIGURE 4.2

The Disappearing Quorum

The Speaker: On this question the yeas are 161, the nays 2.

Mr. Crisp: No quorum.

The Speaker: The Chair directs the Clerk to record the following names of members present and refusing to vote [applause on the Republican side].

Mr. Crisp: I appeal—[applause on the Democratic side]—I appeal the decision of the Chair.

The Speaker [calling off the names of the Democratic members who were present but not voting]: Mr. Blanchard, Mr. Bland, Mr. Blount, Mr. Breckenridge, of Arkansas, Mr. Breckenridge, of Kentucky.

Mr. Breckenridge, of Kentucky: I deny the power of the Speaker and denounce it as revolutionary [applause on the Democratic side which was renewed several times].

Mr. Bland: Mr. Speaker—[applause on the Democratic side].

The Speaker: The House shall be in order.

Mr. Bland: I am responsible to my constituents for the way in which I vote, not to the Speaker of the House [applause].

The Speaker: Mr. Brookshire, Mr. Bullock, Mr. Bynum, Mr. Carlisle, Mr. Chipman, Mr. Clements, Mr. Clunie, Mr. Compton.

Mr. Compton: I protest against the conduct of the chair in calling my name.

The Speaker [proceeding]: Mr. Covert, Mr. Crisp, Mr. Culberson, of Texas [hisses on the Democratic side], Mr. Cummings, Mr. Edmunds, Mr. Enloe, Mr. Fithian, Mr. Goodnight, Mr. Hare, Mr. Hatch, Mr. Hayes.

Mr. Hayes: I appeal from any decision, so far as I am concerned.

The Speaker [continuing]: Mr. Holman, Mr. Lawler, Mr. Lee, Mr. McAdoo, Mr. McCreary.

Mr. McCreary: I deny your right, Mr. Speaker, to count me as present, and I desire to read from the parliamentary law on that subject.

The Speaker: The Chair is making a statement of fact that the gentleman from Kentucky is present. Does he deny it? [laughter and applause on the Republican side].

Source: Peters (1997, 63–64).

"The making of laws is the main function of a legislative body. To that end all other things . . . are subordinate" (Peters 1997, 67). In addition to counting all present members for a quorum, the new rules reduced the number of members required for a quorum to 100, allowed the Speaker to ignore certain dilatory motions, and established other innovations in scheduling legislation.

Speaker Joseph Cannon matched Reed's style with centralized control that earned him the nickname "Czar." Cannon used committee assignments to reward friends and punish enemies and used the Rules Committee and the power of recognition to control the legislative agenda. Cannon used his powers to push policies he favored, especially the tariff. Eventually Cannon alienated a large enough number of members of his own party that a group of Democrats and insurgent Republicans rebelled against his leadership and stripped him of some of his powers (most important, his control over the Rules Committee). This revolt ushered in a period in which the legislative process was controlled by the Democratic caucus. For the next decade all bills had to be approved by the party caucus and committees were basically rubber stamps. This period of centralized control ended in the early 1920s, when committees became the center of legislative activity.

Joseph G. Cannon. Courtesy of the Center for Legislative Archives of the National Archives and Records Administration.

The next major reform effort came in 1946. Congress responded to extensive public criticism that the balance of institutional power had shifted too far toward the president and that Congress was no longer an effective lawmaking body. The reforms were ambitious and far reaching. They rationalized committee jurisdictions, cut the number of committees from forty-eight to nineteen in the House and from thirty-three to fifteen in the Senate, created a comprehensive budget process (which was never fully implemented and lasted only three years), required registration of lobbyists, established expectations for greater oversight of the executive branch, and enhanced the information resources of Congress by expanding the number of committee staffers (staff quadrupled between 1946 and 1966). While these changes had a strong centralizing effect, the actual impact on the committee system was not as substantial as it may first appear. As David King points out, for example, in most cases the committee jurisdictions that were written into the rules simply codified existing practices, rather than changing anything (1997, 62).

While the 1946 reforms centralized the legislative process and enhanced the collective decisionmaking capacity of the institution by eliminating committees and expanding support staff, Congress was still dominated by committee and subcommittee chairs who controlled their pieces of policy turf. This feudal arrangement had important policy consequences in the 1950s and 1960s, especially for civil rights legislation that was stalled or killed by segregationist Southern Democrats. The biggest obstacle was the Rules Committee, which was chaired by the conservative Virginian and segregationist Howard Smith and controlled by a coalition of Republicans and southern Democrats. This committee, which served as the "traffic cop" for all legislation before it reaches the floor, was the graveyard for much progressive legislation. President Kennedy, with the assistance of Speaker Sam Rayburn, helped solve that problem by expanding the size of the Rules Committee from twelve to fifteen members in 1961 (this gave the liberals a one-vote majority on the committee).

In 1965 Congress established another joint committee to examine the lawmaking process, in response to continued concern over inefficiency. This committee made strong recommendations to enhance responsibility and centralization, but the changes were defeated by the committee chairs who feared losing power. However, the recommendations were taken up a few years later and served as the blueprint for the Legislative Reorganization Act of 1970. The unprecedented period of reform that followed over the next seven years proceeded on three tracks: balance of power issues with the president, enhancing responsibility, and improving responsiveness (Rieselbach 1994). Congress was keenly aware that the "imperial presidency" of Richard Nixon had shifted power to the president. To redress this imbalance Congress passed the Budget Impoundment Control Act of 1974 and the War Powers Act of 1973. The former established the budget committees, the Congressional Budget Office, and a new budget process, and severely restricted the president's ability to impound money (which means refusing to spend money that has been appropriated by Congress). The latter established reporting requirements for the presidential use of force and gave Congress the power to withdraw troops after ninety days if they opposed the presidential use of troops.

Reforms that enhanced responsibility limited the seniority norm as the mechanism for choosing committee chairs (this gave party leaders and the caucus more power to select committee chairs who would be more sympathetic to the party's position and thus enhanced the party's collective decisionmaking capacity); limited the number of committee and subcommittee positions that members could hold; and enhanced the power of the Speaker by giving that position control of the Steering and Policy Committee, the ability to appoint Rules Committee members, the power of multiple referral (discussed above), and the ability to create ad hoc task forces and committees on specific issues. The Senate also enhanced its lawmaking power by making it easier to stop filibusters (under the new rule only sixty votes were required to stop a filibuster rather than two-thirds of the senators present and voting, which had meant that sixty-seven votes were required to invoke cloture under the old rule if all senators were present). All of these reforms centralized power and reduced the likelihood of the collective dilemma.

At the same time, however, the reforms of the 1970s made Congress more responsive, thus pushing the institution in the opposite direction from the one outlined above. These reforms decentralized the legislative process through the 1973 "subcommittee bill of rights," which shifted power from committee chair to subcommittee chairs on scheduling, staffing, and control over budgets; "sunshine" laws to open up the legislative process; more recorded votes in committees and on the floor; and an ethics package that included financial disclosure provisions.

The massive reforms of the 1970s did not improve Congress's image. In fact, as noted in Chapter 1, approval ratings for Congress fell to an all-time low in the early 1990s, partly in response to the series of scandals that rocked the institution. Once again, Congress attempted to put its legislative house in order. First, Congress members gave up some perks, shut down the House Bank, limited the franking privilege (whereby members can send mail without postage), and gave up honoraria (in exchange for a sizable pay increase, which got them in more trouble with the public). They also established the Joint Committee on the Organization of Congress, which reported its recommendations on reform late in 1992. The committee suggested a broad range of action on congressional ethics, lobbying reform, congressional compliance with the laws it passes, limiting committee assignments, rationalizing committee jurisdictions, and creating a two-year budget and appropriations cycle. However, none of its major recommendations was enacted before the 1994 elections (the House managed to pass one measure that applied ten labor laws to the House, but not the Senate, see Evans and Oleszek 1997, 74).

The Republicans campaigned on a reform platform in 1994, based on the argument that the Democratic Party, which had controlled the House for forty years, had lost touch with the American people. The "Contract with America"—a set of promises by the Republican House candidates about what they would do if elected—contained eight reforms that would be passed on the first day of Congress: (1) apply all workplace laws to Congress, (2) provide for an independent audit of House finances, (3) reduce the number of House Committees (by three, as it turned out) and cut the number of committee staff by one-third, (4) limit the terms of committee chairs (to six years), (5) abolish proxy voting, (6) require that committee meetings be open to the public, (7) require a three-fifths vote in the House to pass tax increases, and (8) adopt baseline budgeting (Evans and Oleszek 1997, 83–84). The Republicans passed all of these and more (except for the three-fifths requirement for tax increases, which was killed in the Senate). A partial list of the other changes includes giving the Speaker more control over committee assignments, abolishing joint referral of legislation to committees; giving the Speaker an eight-year term limit; giving chairs the power to appoint subcommittee chairs; limiting members to two full-committee assignments, four subcommittee assignments, and one chair of a committee or subcommittee; abolishing the right of delegates to vote on the floor of the House; getting rid of commemorative legislation (symbolic bills like those designating "National Morticians Day" or "National Know Your Cholesterol Month"); promising more open rules (allowing amendments); giving the minority party the right to have at least one vote on their preferred version of all legislation;[4] banning non-emergency provisions in emergency bills; and requiring that the *Congressional Record* reflect what was actually said on the floor of the House (rather than permitting members to edit their remarks, as had been the previous practice). Congress also passed a tough lobbying reform bill that required those who attempt to influence Congress and the executive branch to register and disclose the nature of their activities, and a gift ban that barred members from accepting any gifts (other than small promotional items from the district such as caps and T-shirts), although some free trips are still allowed if the member makes a speech or participates in a charitable activity.

The 1990s reforms, like those of the 1970s, had a mixed impact on the likelihood of the collective dilemma. However, the most important effects of the 1970s reforms were to decentralize Congress and make it more responsive, and thus more susceptible to the collective dilemma, whereas the 1990s reforms had the opposite effect (overall they centralized authority, enhanced collective decision-making, and strengthened responsibility). But Gingrich's push for centralized control derailed after the 1998 midterm elections, as Republicans were reeling when the Democrats picked up House seats (it was the first time since 1934 that the president's party had done so). Gingrich resigned in November 1998, and after Speaker designate Bob Livingston followed suit in December, the Republican Caucus chose the little-known Dennis Hastert (R–Ill.) to be Speaker. In picking Hastert, House Republicans were intentionally foregoing the sort of strong leadership style that Gingrich represented, opting instead for a middle-ground candidate known for his moderate style.

The purpose of this brief history of congressional reform is to identify a general pattern in which Congress periodically acts to centralize control over the legislative procedure to enhance lawmaking capacity and reduce the likelihood of the collective dilemma. In the periods between reforms, there is an inexorable tendency to decentralize control as members pursue their preference for responsiveness over responsibility. When the lawmaking capacity of the institution is sufficiently compromised that outside criticism is intense enough that members fear electoral retribution, they are compelled to act (see Dodd, 1986, for a similar view on institutional change). Unfortunately, the reforms do not always have their intended effects and often they fail to address the underlying collective dilemma (or in some cases they make it worse). In the next section we examine proposed (and enacted) reforms that do (or have done)more harm than good.

Over time, members begin to chafe against centralized control, and eventually conclude that centralization no longer meets their needs. At this point, Congress tends to enact reforms that distribute power more equally throughout the institution. We outline this pattern in Figure 4.3, beginning with the Reed Reforms in 1880, which concentrated power in the hands of the Speaker. In 1910, members revolted against Speaker Cannon, leading to an era in which power shifted from the Speaker to the party caucuses and then to committee chairs. In 1946, because of concern that Congress had been unable to match the institutional strength of the presidency (particularly during World War II, when Congress was largely irrelevant), the reforms represented an attempt to rationalize the committee structure and give Congress more of an institutional capacity to counter presidential influence. The cycle repeated in the 1960s and 1970s, when, once again, dissatisfaction with Congress's ability to legislate—and especially because of opposition to the entrenched power of committee chairs—led to reforms that distributed power more evenly once again (with the "subcommittee bill of rights," and reforms tying committee chairs more closely to the views of the party caucuses).

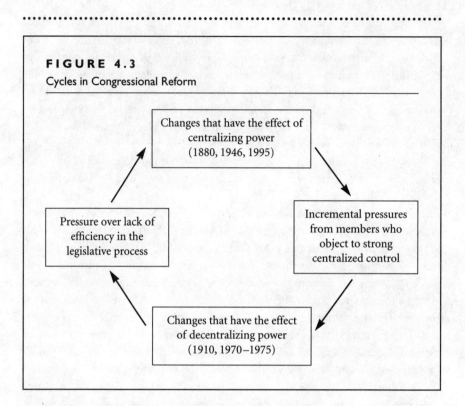

FIGURE 4.3
Cycles in Congressional Reform

Proposed and Recent Reforms and the Collective Dilemma

There is a broad range of ill-advised reforms that we could discuss. The five we have chosen—new electoral rules to provide better descriptive representation, the balanced budget amendment, term limits, the line item veto, and cuts in committee staff—share several elements. All but the first were part of the 1994 "Contract with America." The latter four either would have no impact on the collective dilemma or would make it worse, and none addresses any of the underlying fundamental problems in the American political system. The first, addressing issues of descriptive representation, has some potential to lessen the collective dilemma, but the required institutional remedies are too dramatic to gain substantial political support.

Of the five we discuss, only the cuts in committee staff were in place in 1998. The other four met different fates. Majority-minority districts, as a tool to enhance descriptive representation, were struck down by the Supreme Court, and the other proposals we discuss are unlikely to be implemented. The constitutional amendment to impose term limits on members of Congress was not strongly supported by the leadership and met a relatively swift death in the House; the most votes the amendment received was 227 in the House (63 votes short of the two-thirds necessary for a constitutional amendment). A subsequent attempt to impose term limits on members of Congress through state law was struck down by the Supreme Court (*U.S. Term Limits, Inc. v. Thornton*, 514 U.S. 779 [1995]). The balanced budget amendment passed the House, but failed by one vote in the Senate. The line item veto had the most interesting fate. It passed by a huge 294 to 134 margin in the House and 69 to 29 in the Senate, but then languished in the conference committee for nearly a year before finally passing in April 1996 (it went into effect in January 1997). However, the Supreme Court struck down the law in 1998, saying that it violated the "presentment clause" of the Constitution (*Clinton v. City of New York*, 1998).

Efforts to Promote Descriptive Representation

The primary mechanism for enhancing descriptive representation in Congress, as noted above, was the creation of majority-minority districts in 1992. However, the Supreme Court has ruled that this approach denies white voters "equal protection of the laws," as guaranteed in the 14th Amendment, and therefore is unconstitutional (at least when race is the "predominant factor" drawing the district lines). Therefore, we do not discuss the merits or problems associated with racial redistricting, but rather outline the debates surrounding alternative electoral institutions, such as proportional representation (PR) or cumulative voting, which may provide a stronger voice for minority interests in a majority rule political system (Guinier 1994; Lijphart 1998). There is also evidence that more women gain legislative seats in PR systems than single-member district systems such as the U.S. system (Zimmerman and Rule 1998, 7).

Cumulative voting works in the following fashion: Members of the legislature are elected from multimember districts in which voters have one vote per legislative seat. Voters can allocate their votes among the candidates in any proportion, including "plumping" their votes by casting them all for one candidate. So if there were four House members being elected in your state, you could place all four of your votes for one candidate, three for one and one for another, or any combination you preferred. Thus, minorities who comprised at least 1/nth of the district (where *n* is the number of legislative seats) should in theory always be able to elect at least one of their preferred candidates. This electoral arrangement has received some attention in the popular press and among political scientists as a way of providing more descriptive representation for minorities without having to redraw district lines. Advocates of the technique also argue that it facilitates the building of biracial coalitions (Issacharoff and Pildes 1996, 10).

However, there are several potential problems with cumulative voting. It is relatively complex and will produce voter confusion, at least in the short-term. It will shift power to groups of voters with higher turnout rates (elderly, wealthy, highly educated whites) because they would be able to influence elections in a broader geographic area. It would most likely benefit minorities of the right, who are more easily mobilized. Multimember districts in which the cumulative voting would occur would be so large as to virtually do away with the concept of geographic representation that is so central to American politics (Morrill 1996, 4–5). Finally, it could produce a less stable, more fractured political system (Forest 1996, 10). One other unintended effect often not mentioned by proponents of the system: Republicans are likely to benefit from cumulative voting even more than they did from the creation of black-majority districts. If Republicans "plump" their votes, they should be able to elect candidates roughly in proportion to their population, just as minorities would. For example, in Chilton County, Alabama, an area where Republicans rarely won local office, three of the seven commission seats went to Republicans when cumulative voting was adopted. Furthermore, minorities would need to construct powerful slating organizations to limit the supply of candidates, or risk splitting their limited voting power. In Centre, Alabama, another community that tried cumulative voting, a black city councilman was elected when the plan was implemented in 1988. But in 1992, he had black competition and the city council reverted to being all-white (Van Biema 1994, 43). The practice is clearly not a panacea for minority representation.

Unlike cumulative voting, proportional representation (PR) systems are already used throughout the world. Evidence shows that PR systems and parliamentary governments are better for minority representation than winner-take-all elections and presidential governments. Proportional representation systems are fairer than plurality systems, they are more inclusive, they promote power sharing and consociational democracy, and thus, they provide a greater voice for ethnic and racial minorities. Shugart and Carey point out three characteristics of presidential governments that are especially bad for racially or ethnically diverse societies: "temporal rigidity, majoritarianism, and dual democratic legitimacy" (1992, 28–43). The worst of these is the winner-take-all quality of majoritarianism in a presidential system; minorities that fear permanent majority tyranny will have little incentive to buy into a zero-sum game.

However, this view is not universally held. Supporters of plurality elections point out a range of problems with PR that are similar to the drawbacks of cumulative voting (Lardeyret 1991; Horowitz 1991; Barkan 1995). These critics point out that large, broad-based, and ethnically diverse political parties in a plurality system are more likely to promote stable, democratic politics than politically extreme, racially homogeneous, regional parties that may be produced in a PR system.

Proportional representation systems also tend to elect more women than do single-member district systems, something that enhances descriptive representation. Wilma Rule writes, "Electoral arrangements are not neutral; they are the means used to exclude or include groups. The arrangements are amenable to change faster than social biases and other barriers to women's election opportunity and fair representation" (1994, 689). She demonstrates that of the twenty-seven "long established democracies," the nine with the highest proportion of women in the lower houses of parliament are all PR systems. Of the next seventeen, eight are single-member and nine are PR. The mean percentage of women parliament members for the PR nations was 18.4 percent, compared to 10.1 percent in the single-member nations. Even more telling are the figures on the upper and lower houses of parliament in Australia, Japan, and Germany: these nations use PR in the upper house, where an average of 25.3 percent of members are women, whereas the lower houses use single-member districts (or "small districts" in the case of Japan) and have an average of 7 percent women. Similar evidence from the United States shows that in the fifteen states that have multimember districts for their state legislatures, 21.8 percent of the legislators are women, compared to 12.4 percent in the thirty-five states with single-member districts. While the causal mechanisms that produce these relationship are still not entirely clear, electoral systems are not neutral when it comes to electing women. (See Rule and Zimmerman 1994, for a more complete analysis of these and other data on the representation of women and minorities in different types of electoral systems.)

The skeptical reader may argue that these comparisons are interesting, but irrelevant for the American case because practical politics dictate that PR or alternative electoral systems will never be implemented in the United States. However, twenty-two municipalities used some type of proportional system between 1915 and 1964 (Weaver 1986, 141) and many jurisdictions continue to employ multimember districts that could easily be converted to cumulative voting. Even if practical politics seem to preclude certain policies, it is useful to consider the full range of theoretical options for improving descriptive representation.

While we do not endorse the adoption of cumulative voting or PR electoral mechanisms, some of the other efforts to enhance descriptive representation outlined above, such as the direct recruitment of minorities and women to run for office and the creation of electoral districts that enhance the opportunity to elect more minorities, are desirable because they decrease the likelihood of the collective dilemma. Members elected from majority-minority districts are in practice more likely to adopt a biracial approach to politics that balances the interests of their racially diverse constituents (Canon forthcoming). Also, legislatures that have large numbers of women are more likely to be sensitive to a broader range of issues that are of interest to women than legislatures that have small numbers of women (Thomas and Wilcox 1998). Therefore, these efforts to enhance descriptive representation make legislatures more responsive to a broader range of issues that are in the collective interest of their constituents.

Term Limits

There are many reasons to oppose term limitations for members of Congress. Most obvious is the loss of many of the nation's top leaders. It takes many years to learn how Congress works and to master the technical details of complex issues. The senior members of Congress play a central role in institutional maintenance and the heavy lifting of the lawmaking process. New members who are trying to shore up their electoral bases are not as likely to dedicate substantial time to the hard work of lawmaking and coalition building. Workhorses such as Senator John McCain (R–Ariz.) and Representative Henry Waxman (D–Calif.) are not easily replaced. Removing experienced legislators would simply transfer power to unelected congressional staff and bureaucrats. These people—who have virtually no accountability—would form the new power centers of the permanent government.

Equally troubling is the patronizing attitude about voters implicit in the term-limitation movement. The message is that voters cannot be trusted to elect their own representatives. Voters seem to be saying, "Stop me before I vote again." The problem is that most people see term limits as a way to limit the influence of *other people's* representatives: despite the public's low opinion of Congress, as we noted in Chapter 1, most people continue to think their own representative is doing a good job. As such, term limits violate the fundamental principle behind geographic representation, that people outside a congressional district may not determine who residents of that district may elect.

No matter how much people in California or Utah may detest Representative Bob Barr (R–Ga.) or Senator Ted Kennedy (D–Mass.) and want them out of office, that decision is not theirs to make; it rests, rather, with the voters of Georgia's 7th congressional district and the state of Massachusetts, respectively. We recognize, to be sure, that "outsiders" can still exert some influence in local races by, for example, making campaign contributions to candidates across the country (in fact, federal courts have consistently rejected campaign finance laws that prohibit contributions from outside the state or congressional district). But that is quite different from declaring that voters may not choose their own representative simply because he or she has already served an arbitrarily set number of terms.

The arguments in favor of term limits fall apart when subjected to scrutiny; they are based more on emotion than reason. According to proponents, term limits would be beneficial because they would introduce new blood into the institution, would reduce the influence of special interests, and would make members more responsive to "the people" than to their own power interests. Unfortunately, there is simply no evidence that term limits would actually solve any of these problems.

Whatever problems there are with Congress, they are not due to the lack of new members. Even with a reelection rate of 97 percent between 1986 and 1990 (the highest success rate in history), 129 new members were elected to the U.S. House in that span. With the huge freshman classes in 1993 (110) and 1995 (86), more than half of the House members had served for four years or less on the first day of the 105th Congress in January 1997 (132 of the 227 Republicans and 102 of the 208 Democrats, or 56.1 percent of the total). Less than a third of House members had served more than ten years (31.9 percent). Turnover is also relatively high in the Senate, where 43 members had served for one term (six years) or less at the start of the 105th Congress. Only 31 senators had served more than two terms (the typical proposed term limit for the Senate).

The idea that term-limited legislators would be less beholden to special interests is unfounded as well. Without campaign finance reform, members would still have to rely on PACs for campaign funds. While many powerful special interests oppose term limits—because they understand how the current system works—there is no doubt that they would quickly adapt and gain just as much access and influence in a term-limited legislature as they have now. In fact, members may become *more* dependent on lobbyists, who would have an advantage in expertise over inexperienced legislators. Indeed, evidence from California shows that term limits can do more harm than good. California adopted strict term limits for state offices in 1990, and by 1998 the entire state legislature had turned over as term-limited legislators were forced to retire. The results were not what proponents had hoped for. The amount spent by lobbying groups rose from $116 million in 1991 to $144 million in 1997; campaign expenditures for state legislative candidates nearly doubled, from $54 million in 1989–1990 to $106 million in 1995–1996; and legislative incumbents outspent challengers by almost twenty to one in the Assembly and fifty to one in the State Senate (California Secretary of State 1997). A *Los Angeles Times* editorial noted the disappointing results in 1998:

> More than ever, Assembly members' attention is focused on partisan politics, fundraising and what they will do when termed out. The logical step up is to move to the Senate. Because each Senate district is composed of two Assembly districts, there is often tension between the two members over which will be better positioned to move up when the Senate seat comes open. The fresh blood in the Legislature has produced

some creative thinking and a few new ideas. . . . But usually, the new members dis-
cover that their "new" ideas have been tried before and have failed. Legislating, they
find, involves skills of give and take, of fine-tuning details, of knowing when to force
an issue or quietly retreat (*Los Angeles Times* 1998, A7).

All of these concerns indicate that term limits would exacerbate the collective
dilemma, without addressing the underlying problems. In any event, it is unlikely
that Congress will be able to muster the two-thirds votes in both chambers that
would be necessary to pass a term-limit amendment to the Constitution (the
Amendment would then have to be ratified by three-fourths (thirty-eight) of the
states before it would be added to the Constitution).

Balanced Budget Amendment

A balanced budget amendment to the constitution would require that expenditures are not greater than revenues in any given year. The version that was proposed in 1995 (H.J. Res. 1) would have allowed deficits if three-fifths of both
houses of Congress agreed; the requirement could also be suspended during
wartime by a simple majority vote of the House and Senate. The debt ceiling was
to be set at the then-current level and could not be exceeded unless there was a
three-fifths vote of both houses, and any tax increases would require the same
three-fifths margin. A balanced budget amendment was first proposed in Congress in 1936 and came up regularly in the next few decades. In 1982, it passed the
Senate, but failed in the House by forty-seven votes. The amendment was wildly
popular with a public that could easily identify with the necessity of balancing
budgets, and it appeared to have the critical mass needed for approval in Congress. Budget deficits of mind-numbing proportions (nearly $300 billion at their
peak, with an accumulated addition of more than $3 trillion in total debt since
1981) seemed to defy legislative solution and members of Congress were feeling
the heat to do something. As a centerpiece of the "Contract with America," the
Republican leadership made it their top priority.

The Republican version of the amendment ran aground on the provision that
required a three-fifths vote to raise taxes (it fell 37 votes short of the 290 needed
for a Constitutional amendment). However, a Democratic substitute, which was
identical to the "Contract" version with the exception of stripping the tax measure, sailed through the House by a 300 to 132 vote on the twenty-second day of
the session. However, the amendment failed by a single vote in the Senate.

There are numerous technical arguments in favor of and opposed to the balanced budget amendment;[5] however, the issue that concerns us here is its impact

on the separation of powers and Congress's lawmaking capacity. After noting that constitutional amendments almost always have unintended structural consequences, Kathleen Sullivan states: "[A]dvocates of the balanced budget amendment focus on claims that elimination of the deficit will help investment and growth. But they ignore the structural consequences of shifting fiscal power from Congress to the president or the courts" (1997, 65). The taxing and spending powers are clearly granted to Congress in Article I of the Constitution, but a constitutional requirement to keep the budget in balance would create huge interbranch battles over defining the deficit. Whose economic forecasts would be used when projecting whether the budget would be in balance: the Congressional Budget Office or the Office of Management and Budget? What happens if both sets of forecasts are off? Does the president have to impound the money? Undoubtedly, the Supreme Court would get dragged in to settle the disputes. It is safe to say that the Framers did not envision the Supreme Court writing the nation's budget. Congressional abdication of its lawmaking responsibility is not an acceptable solution to the collective dilemma, nor to the nation's economic problems. In any case, pressure for the amendment evaporated when the federal budget ran a *surplus* in fiscal year 1998 (the first surplus in three decades), with more surpluses projected over the next ten years.

Line Item Veto

Nearly every president in the twentieth century sought a line item veto as a tool to restrain a fiscally irresponsible Congress. The Republican Congress finally gave the president his wish in fulfilling one of the promises of the "Contract with America." The law gave the president the power to cancel any discretionary appropriation, any new spending item, or any "limited tax benefit" (that affected fewer than one hundred people or entities) within five days of the law's passage. If the item is canceled, Congress has the power to pass a "disapproval bill" by a simple majority vote, which can in turn be vetoed by the president (this would then require the standard two-thirds vote in both houses to override the president's veto). Proponents of the line item veto argue that it is needed to restrain wasteful "pork barrel spending" and to restore the president's true veto power, which has been virtually eliminated by the large "omnibus" bills that require the president to veto the entire thing (which would often mean shutting down large parts of the government), or allow the pork to slip through (Gimpel 1996, 50–54).

While Congress certainly passes plenty of pork, the proportion of spending that is "waste" is often greatly exaggerated. As the saying goes, "Pork is in the eye of the beholder." That is, one person's "pork" is another person's "essential spending." Furthermore, the line item veto is not a very useful tool for reducing spending because it only affects about one-sixth of the total budget (discretionary spending). For our purposes, the crucial point is that the line item veto could make the collective dilemma worse by encouraging members to act on district interests. It is possible that members would pass more district-based spending measures for symbolic purposes, knowing that the president will exercise discipline on the budget. This would allow the reelection-minded members to go to their constituents and tell them that they fought the good fight, but that the stingy president vetoed the goodies for the district. While the most egregious of the wasteful pork items could be deterred by the line item veto (national attention would be focused on the members' waste), it is unlikely that responsible behavior would generally be encouraged by the line item veto.

The most compelling argument against the line item veto, from our perspective, is that it represents an abdication of authority and responsibility on Congress's part and a significant shift of power to the executive. This undermines the lawmaking capacity of Congress and would have a long-term detrimental effect on the institution. As noted above, the Supreme Court ruled that the law was unconstitutional; therefore, if the line item veto is to become the law of the land, it will have to be done through a constitutional amendment (which is not very likely to pass).

Cuts in Committee Staff

Since the 1946 Legislative Reform Act, Congress has recognized the need for sources of information that are independent of the executive branch. The expansion of committee staff has served as an important check on presidential power and has provided Congress with essential knowledge needed to formulate legislation. However, in the early 1990s, cutting the "bloated congressional bureaucracy became an easy bone to throw to the hungry and disgruntled public. In the last presidential debate of the 1992 campaign, President Bush and Bill Clinton engaged in a "bidding war" to see who would seek the deeper cuts in congressional staff (Clinton promised a 25 percent cut and Bush countered with 33 percent) (Mann and Ornstein 1992, 66). The Joint Committee also sought deep cuts, with Senator Boren (D–Okla.) and Representative Dreier (R–Calif.) leading the charge. Boren argued, "I believe our bureaucracy has become an entangling bureaucracy rather than a staff which serves our needs as it should. I think we would be more efficient and effective with a leaner staff, at least 25 percent smaller than it is now, more effectively targeted and with a committee system that works" (quoted in Evans and Oleszek 1997, 67). The Brookings/American Enterprise report on congressional reform recognized that some cuts would probably be a good thing, but provided a voice of caution that went unheeded:

> One problem with across-the-board staff cuts is immediately apparent: they would be counterproductive. The more efficiently run, already over-burdened areas would be hardest hit by such cuts. Rather than promoting efficiency, cuts would be likely to increase inefficiency and staff turnover and further weaken the institution. . . . [M]ajor cuts in committee and subcommittee staffs would almost certainly make Congress more dependent on the executive branch and on interest groups for information and guidance (Mann and Orenstein 1992, 67).

We agree. The cuts in committee staff that were adopted at the beginning of the 104th Congress reduced the lawmaking capacity of Congress and increased the likelihood of the collective dilemma. This "reform" indicates the damage that can be done when members listen to public opinion polls rather than do what is in the best interests of the institution. Cutting committee staff is one of the clearest indicators of members' preference for responsiveness over responsibility: members' personal staffs that handle constituency service and casework were not touched by the reforms of the 104th Congress.

Three of the reforms discussed here that were not the law of the land at the end of the 1990s—term limits, the balanced budget amendment, and the line item veto—are good examples of why constitutional amendments should not be used to address passing political fads. The underlying conditions that make a problem seem so serious can change quickly. The need for term limits, if it was ever present, has been undermined by the high turnover rates of the three elections in the mid-1990s. The balanced budget amendment and line item veto were both driven by concern about the seemingly endless budget deficits. However, projections in 1998 called for a $100 billion surplus in fiscal year 1999. Support among Republicans in Congress for the line item veto also waned after the president lined out eighty-two items in eleven laws, including some of their pet projects. Changes that are written into the Constitution permanently alter the institutional balance of power (unless another amendment is passed, which is extremely unlikely) and therefore should be used very sparingly as a tool of congressional reform. In Chapter 5 we examine reforms that would "do the right thing" rather than the expedient or popular thing.

5

....

An Agenda for Reform

*Coming to Terms with
the Collective Dilemma*

•••

In Chapter 4, we argued that many popular reforms would serve mainly to weaken Congress and transfer power to the president and bureaucracy. Like the medical practice of bloodletting used several hundred years ago, these reforms would attempt to rid impurities from Congress by opening wounds and letting the institution bleed. The patient cannot be cured by making it sicker. A central goal of reforms must be to maintain the separation of powers and system of checks and balances, while enhancing Congress's collective decisionmaking capacity.

There is no way to eliminate the collective dilemma. The clash between individual, district-based interests and the national and institutional collective good is simply inherent in an open democratic system premised on local representation. Enhancing collective decisionmaking implies more centralization, or increasing the power of party leaders. But this path to reform is no panacea. Newt Gingrich, when he assumed the Speakership in January 1995, was likened to Joe Cannon, one of the most powerful Speakers in the twentieth century. Yet his influence collapsed during the course of the 104th Congress as the public held the G.O.P. responsible for government shutdowns and attacks on favored programs. Gingrich contributed to his own weakness by what the public perceived as a strident and overbearing style and his ethics problems (he used his PAC to illegally support federal candidates and was censured and fined by the House), but the problems of congressional accountability go deeper than these issues. No Speaker, no matter what resources he or she brings to the table, can compete with the president for democratic legitimacy or control of the country's agenda. Furthermore, as Ronald Peters points out, centralization comes at a price. In reference to Speaker Jim Wright's use of restrictive rules in the House, Peters wrote, "When the rules are used for partisan political purpose, they derogate from the House's capacity to deliberate. Control supersedes comity, and the legislative body is damaged at its core" (1997, 270). Furthermore, the value of a centralized decisionmaking process depends on the degree to which there is consensus about the collective goals that will be pursued. An efficient lawmaking institution is fine, as long as everyone agrees with what it decides to do. To see that this is true, ask yourself whether you would be willing to grant Congress both a strong Speaker and carte blanche to enact legislation, before you know whether Newt Gingrich or Bernie Sanders (an Independent from Vermont, and a socialist) will be Speaker. If you are not sure you will like what Congress may do, then you will insist on protections to make sure that you have a chance to influence (or, at a minimum, obstruct) legislative action.

Nor is decentralization the answer. As described in the previous chapter, reforms adopted in the mid-1970s dramatically increased the influence of rank-and-file members and increased institutional responsiveness, but at the price of inefficiency in the lawmaking process.

And, as we have noted many times throughout this book, there is no way to maximize *deliberative lawmaking capabilities* and *public responsiveness* at the same time: if Congress is to deliberate and have the capability to buck public opinion when the "collective good" requires it, then there must be some sort of insulation between members and the public. This necessarily implies fewer access points through which outside interests can press their case. Critics of Congress argue that this insulation already exists, but selectively, because members pay too much attention to what their big contributors want and too little to what is in the public interest.

A final caveat before we suggest our reforms: procedural reforms by themselves do not offer a foolproof solution to the problems faced by Congress (although they can certainly mitigate the collective dilemma). While it is too early fully to identify the consequences of the reforms instituted by the G.O.P. majority in the 104th Congress, it *is* possible to note that many of the changes have not had the anticipated effects that the originators hoped for. As one example, beginning with the 104th Congress, Republicans adopted a rule limiting the Speaker to four consecutive terms and committee chairs to three consecutive terms. The intent was ostensibly to limit the power of entrenched seniority (as symbolized by the long tenure of Congressman John Dingell [D–Mich.], who parlayed his chairmanship of the House Energy and Commerce Committee into one of the most powerful and enduring legislative fiefdoms in congressional history) and make it easier for backbenchers to have more influence over legislation. But accounts suggest that the reforms have generated huge levels of uncertainty, as senior committee chairs contemplate their forced removal beginning in 2001 and junior members jockey for position. As one journalist put it:

> With 13 committee chairmanships and dozens of subcommittee spots up for grabs in 2000, the politics of seniority have given way to the politics of savagery. Junior Republicans, once content to toil on the Merchant Marine subcommittee, are rushing to fill the vacuum, while senior members, faced with losing their committees, are contemplating either retiring or appropriating even bigger fiefdoms" (Grann 1998, 12).

Ironically, the reforms have sped the exodus of senior legislators, who find the prospect of moving from committee chair to rank-and-file status distasteful, which is not something that the Republican leaders anticipated or wanted.

So what is to be done? We propose reforms that will lead to increased electoral competition and make the campaign finance system better serve collective interests, provide some insulation for members by encouraging the use of bipartisan commissions when they are needed and rescinding some of the "sunshine" reforms of the 1970s, improve Congress's deliberative capacity, and help educate the public about Congress's legislative responsibilities.

Campaign Finance Reform

There are two reasons why we see campaign finance reform as central to any effort to mitigate the policy and institutional dilemmas that legislators face. First, few reforms would do more to enhance public confidence in Congress: the pervasive view that the current system is fundamentally corrupt will, at some point, erode the basic legitimacy of Congress as a lawmaking body. A bipartisan review of congressional reform, conducted by the Brookings Institution and American Enterprise Institute, concluded that, "No effort to reform Congress and revitalize its role in national policy making can possibly succeed without a fundamental restructuring of the campaign finance system. And no aspect of Congress contributes more to its low public repute than the means by which election campaigns are financed" (Mann and Ornstein 1992, 62). We outlined some of the problems in Chapter 3: the need to spend vast amounts of time raising funds, which diverts members from substantive legislative duties; the presence of huge and increasing individual, corporate, and union soft money donations, which make a mockery of contribution limits; the difficulty that challengers face in trying to build credible campaigns; and the decentralizing forces that reward individual entrepreneurial activity at the expense of party organization and discipline. We are less concerned about the connection between interested money (e.g., PAC donations) and legislative outcomes; although many reform initiatives are premised on the "quid pro quo" problem and seek to drive private money out of the process altogether, in our view this is not the central problem.

Second, our recommended reforms would reduce the amount of time members now spend on raising funds, and strengthen the forces that bind members together in pursuit of common goals. At the same time, what we propose would additionally create increased competition and accountability in congressional races. The key to a viable electoral system is its ability to foster competition and accountability. If voters have realistic and viable choices in campaigns, and thereby have an instrument to hold candidates and parties accountable for collective decisions, that alone will mitigate many of the problems that beset the current system. More important, choices and accountability solve problems without intruding upon legitimate concerns regarding First Amendment considerations of free speech and association.

Our recommendations are to (1) eliminate soft money by requiring political parties to raise *all* of their funds according to the current limits on "hard money"; (2) increase the amount that political parties can contribute directly to candidates (currently $20,000 for House candidates and up to $27,500 for the Senate) to $250,000 for the House and up to $1 million for the Senate (with the Senate limits depending on the number of voters in each state), and index the limits to inflation; and (3) encourage broader public participation in campaigns by providing for a federal tax credit for individual contributions of up to $100 per election cycle. Together, these reforms would significantly enhance collective decisionmaking and accountability.

We concede that our recommendations do not comprise a comprehensive package, and that they do not address other important issues (such as how to deal

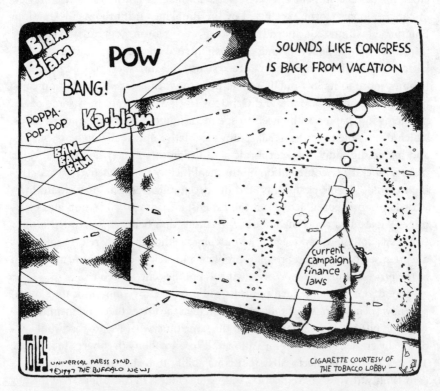

Sounds like Congress is back from vacation. TOLES © 1991 & 1997 the *Buffalo News*. Reprinted with permission of UNIVERSAL PRESS SYNDICATE. All rights reserved.

with independent expenditures). The reforms we suggest are not new, and all have been recommended at either the state or federal level by other reform advocates (including the League of Women Voters, the Brookings Institution, Citizens' Research Foundation, and the Center for Responsive Politics). Nevertheless, we believe that as a starting point our proposals can resolve some of the more serious problems that undermine Congress as an institution and mitigate the difficulties of acting in the collective interest.

Banning Soft Money

There is no plausible justification for soft money, at least as it has evolved. As we noted in Chapter 3, Congress originally allowed for soft money donations out of a desire to foster grassroots party activities. That objective, though, has been completely eviscerated as political parties learned how to maneuver around the intent of the law. What was originally envisioned as a way for parties to pay for voter education programs and get-out-the-vote drives is now a way for parties to raise huge sums of money in unimaginably large chunks to support national ad campaigns.

Apart from those who take a decidedly libertarian view of campaigns—such as the Cato Institute, a Washington, D.C., policy think tank that proposes to completely deregulate campaign finance—almost no one defends soft money, not even those who benefit most from it. We propose a simple solution: require national parties to raise all of their funds through the existing limits on hard money, and prohibit transfers of these funds to state and local parties (Citizens' Research Foundation 1996). Under these rules, individuals may contribute up to $20,000 per election cycle, and corporate and labor union contributions are prohibited. The parties already raise significant funds under the current federal limits, with over $600 million raised in 1995–1996, so this should not significantly constrain their activities (although a significant percentage of that money goes directly back into fund-raising operations).

At the same time, banning soft money will be ineffective without a tightening of the definition of what, exactly, constitutes activity designed to influence federal elections or benefit a candidate (or, what the Federal Election Commission calls "express advocacy"). As currently defined, as long as an advertising campaign does not clearly advocate the election or defeat of a candidate, it can fall under the loosely regulated category of "issue advertising," or speech intended to provide general information about political issues. Yet parties and interest groups have become increasingly adept at creating advertisements that, under any reasonable definition, are campaign ads but are considered issue advertising because they narrowly avoid the explicit characteristics that would make them campaign advertisements. Many states allow corporations and labor unions to contribute to state party organizations, so without a tightening of this rule, what is now soft money would simply be funneled to state organizations. One possible solution, adopted at the state level in Colorado, and included as a provision in the Shays-Meehan and McCain-Feingold campaign finance reform bills, would define federal election activity as anything that identifies a candidate for federal office or is designed to influence an election for a federal office, whether or not it is defined as "express advocacy."

People tend to be instinctively repulsed by reports of huge individual and corporate contributions to political parties: $10 million raised from a single dinner held by the Republican Congressional Campaign Committee in June 1998; the Chairman of Loral Corporation donating over $1 million to Democratic Party committees since 1995, while his company was seeking permission to export satellite technology to China. Soft money benefits the parties and the collective decisionmaking capacity of Congress, to be sure, but it has a demonstrably corrosive effect on the public's confidence in politics and on governmental institutions. The proposal we outline below will enhance the centralizing power of parties, without the corrupting influence of soft money.

Raise Party Contribution Limits

Direct party contributions to candidates now comprise only a trivial percentage of overall spending. In 1996, House and Senate candidates combined spent $638 million. Of that total, only $5.2 million—less than 1 percent of each dollar—came in the form of direct contributions from parties.[1] Under current law, even if parties ran candidates in every House and Senate race and "maxed out" on all of them in the general election campaign (meaning that it contributed the maximum allowable by law), total party contributions from all sources would be less than $10 million.[2]

Candidates, then, simply do not rely on party organizations for anything more than a trivial level of financial support. This gives party leaders very little leverage over legislators, and also prevents parties from offering substantial financial support to challengers. We noted some of the consequences of this problem in Chapter 3: candidates acting independently of their parties, and showing less loyalty than they perhaps would if parties had more stake in individual races.

Significantly raising direct contribution limits would have three consequences. First, it would make parties more effective agents for collective action, since members would rely on them for a meaningful amount of financial support. The prospect of withholding a large contribution gives parties a more effective sanction to control members. Any prospect for control, to be sure, raises the prospect for abuse and legislators may come to fear party leaders who seek to bully them into submission. But parties are, ultimately, agents of their membership and party leaders who stray too far from what their members in Congress want will soon find themselves replaced. Even Newt Gingrich, considered one of the most powerful Speakers of the twentieth century, barely survived a "palace coup" attempt in July 1997: Several members of the Republican House leadership, and a few dozen rank-and-file Republicans, organized an abortive rebellion out of dissatisfaction with Gingrich's management of the House (Koszczuk 1997). He was ousted after the 1998 midterm elections.

Second, raising party limits would provide underfunded candidates—meaning challengers—with a critical source of seed money that would allow them to run more credible campaigns. This, in turn, would create a more competitive electoral environment, since voters would have a viable option to the incumbent. In 1996, the average House challenger spent $286,000, less than half of what the average incumbent spent. In less competitive races (defined as those in which the incumbent received more than 60 percent of the two-party vote), challengers managed to spend only $102,000 on average. Providing these candidates with a potential source of funding that could double or triple their spending would create a larger number of competitive races, and could significantly reduce the incumbency advantage. Providing substantial money to challengers could also enhance the collective lawmaking capacity of Congress by making new incumbents more linked to political parties and more likely to support the party platform. While it is unlikely that this reform would eliminate the candidate-centered nature of today's politics, it should mitigate this tendency to some extent.

So far, we have discussed only the consequences that tend to hurt the interests of existing legislators (by reducing their autonomy with respect to the parties and reducing their incumbency advantage). But there is a third consequence that redounds to the advantage of individual legislators. That advantage is the availability of significant funds from a single source, which frees legislators from the need to raise this money from private sources. Although the larger party contributions would clearly not eliminate the need for individual and PAC fund-raising, members would be free to spend less time on what they regard as a distasteful task. This also increases the collective lawmaking capacity of Congress by providing members with more time for their legislative work.

Tax Credits for Small Individual Contributions

In 1996, a Brookings Institution Forum on campaign finance reform recommended a tax credit for small individual contributions. Their recommendation was to:

> Create a $100 tax credit for in-state contributions to federal candidates of $100 or less. The credit would apply to the first $100 an individual gave to candidates—in other words, $25 given to each of four candidates would result in a $100 credit. It would not apply to large contributions; it would be phased out if an individual gave more than $200 to a candidate (Corrado et al. 1997, 383).

We strongly endorse this option, for two reasons. First, it can have the salutary effect of making candidate and party fund-raising more efficient, since people will presumably be more likely to respond to a solicitation if a contribution ultimately costs them nothing. This can reduce the amount of time candidates have to spend raising money, which produces the benefits outlined above. Second, it can broaden the participatory base of campaigns, by involving more people in the electoral process and making the process more representative.[3] This proposal is designed to raise the institutional standing of Congress in the public's eye, on the theory that more involvement will lead to higher levels of engagement and a sense that people have a stake in controlling Congress.

How much would this program cost? It is hard to say, since under current law federal candidates do not have to itemize contributions of under $200; as a result, we do not know precisely how many people donate $100 or less. What we do know is that in 1995–1996, individuals contributed a total of $158 million to House and Senate candidates in amounts of $200 or less. That figure provides the upper boundary of what the tax refund program would have cost in 1995–1996, although it could be higher if the number of small contributions rises, or lower if the average contribution in this group actually exceeded $100. A rough estimate, then, is approximately $100 million per election cycle.

Taken together, the reforms we propose would strengthen parties, provide for more competition in congressional elections, and broaden public involvement in the campaign process. We have argued throughout this book that it is not possible to *eliminate* the collective dilemma, but it is possible to reduce the pressure of centrifugal forces that push members away from the collective good, and also to eliminate features of the current system that do little but drag Congress down in the public's estimation.

Weakening the Traceability Chain

While this recommendation may be controversial, we argue that Congress will be better able to overcome the collective dilemma if the "traceability chain" is weakened. This means that Congress needs to be more insulated from political pressure in order to do what is in the nation's collective interest. Specifically, the "traceability chain" refers to Douglas Arnold's argument that legislative leaders can enhance the prospects for passing legislation that imposes large and immediate costs on some segment of the population if they use mechanisms that make it less likely that voters will be able to trace the source of the costs to actions taken by individual members of Congress (1990, 100). For example, it may be in the nation's interest to strengthen clean air laws, but companies that pollute will bear large costs for the benefits that will be widely shared by the broader public. Those who bear large, concentrated costs are likely to mobilize against the legislation and punish members who support it, while those who benefit from cleaner air are not as likely to mobilize in favor of the legislation because the benefits are relatively small (and perhaps even undetectable in the short run) and widely dispersed. Therefore, one way to increase the likelihood that legislation that is in the nation's collective interest passes is to provide cover for members who want to do the right thing.

There are many mechanisms that may be used to weaken the traceability chain: omnibus legislation, closed or restrictive rules, delegation of authority to the other branches of government, executive summits, fast-track provisions, bipartisan commissions, and greater secrecy. We discuss the last two in some detail below and briefly describe the others here. Omnibus legislation refers to the huge packages of legislation, such as the 1980 Omnibus Reconciliation Act, the 1986 Tax Reform Act, or 1997 welfare reform, that bundle together many separate provisions. Members are not able to vote on the separate provisions, but must either support or oppose the legislation in a single vote. In such instances, members of Congress can vote for controversial measures that are contained in an overall package that is generally popular. Omnibus legislation is typically protected by closed rules that prohibit amendments to the package, or restrictive rules that severely limit the number and type of amendments that can be offered. This technique clearly enhances Congress's collective lawmaking capacity, but it also is vulnerable to abuse. Members may see omnibus legislation as an opportunity to attach unrelated riders or pet projects, "transition rules" that benefit specific individuals or corporations, or other extraneous measures that would otherwise not pass. Thus, omnibus legislation should not be overused and the leadership should try to make sure that the procedure is not misused.

Congress may also weaken the traceability chain by simply delegating unpleasant tasks to the president, the bureaucracy, the courts, or a regulatory agency (Arnold 1990, 103). For example, in 1970 Congress passed the Clean Air Act, which established certain standards for cleaning up the air, while giving the newly created Environmental Protection Agency (EPA) substantial discretion in enforcing the law. Congress avoided making many of the tough choices because of the collective dilemma and in this instance delegation did not work in the public's interest because the EPA was not very aggressive in enforcing the law (Schoenbrod 1993, chapter 4). However, in other instances, delegation does serve the collective interests. For example, the Federal Reserve Act of 1913, which created the Federal Reserve System, is widely hailed as an important act of delegation that helped stabilize our economic system and provided a strong, independent basis for controlling the nation's monetary system (Kettl 1986).

Delegation of authority to the courts is not as straightforward. In some areas Congress has delegated authority to quasi-judicial agencies, such as the National Labor Relations Board, which oversees the formation of labor unions and negotiations between labor and management. In other instances, Congress has passed vaguely worded statutes that must be interpreted and refined by the courts, as in the areas of gender discrimination or voting rights. In other instances, the Supreme Court has interjected itself into the process, exercising its power of judicial review. In many of these cases, members of Congress have succumbed to the collective dilemma and done what is in their interests rather than the collective interest. For example, when the Supreme Court prohibited school prayer and term limits and allowed flag burning, this served as a check on the majoritarian impulses of Congress (a majority of members also supported a balanced budget amendment, but a two-thirds vote was required for a constitutional amendment). In these instances, in our view, the Court upheld the Constitution and protected the long-term interests of the nation, rather than giving in to short-term political pressures.

However, there are other instances in which the Court should not get involved in policy disputes. For questions that are inherently political, rather than constitutional, the Court should defer to the elected branches when possible. In most instances, the Court is reluctant to enter the "political thicket," but one recent example of judicial activism that has muddied the policy process is in the area of racial redistricting. In a series of confusing cases starting with *Shaw v. Reno* in 1993, the Supreme Court has articulated an ambiguous set of standards that has left redistricting in a state of confusion. In essence, the Court has told state legislatures that race cannot be "the predominant factor" in deciding how to redraw district lines, but it has not told them how race could be used. Given the inherent uncertainty surrounding this question, the representative process would be better served by having legislators battle it out on a state-by-state basis rather than having unelected judges attempt to resolve a collective dilemma that ultimately has no permanent solution.

Presidential/congressional summits are another tool that may be used to promote collective decisionmaking and break logjams created by the collective dilemma. In 1990, President Bush and the Democratically controlled Congress were struggling with how to control the mammoth budget deficits that faced the nation. Congressional leaders did not want to stick their necks out by recommending painful budget cuts or tax increases, and the president felt bound by his campaign pledge of "Read my lips—no new taxes." After some fits and starts, including a rejection by Congress of an initial package, the president and congressional leaders were able to come up with a five-year, $500 billion deficit reduction plan that was approved by a 228 to 200 vote (Schuman 1992, 229). The budget deal may have doomed President Bush's reelection chances (because he broke his "read my lips" pledge), but it placed the budget on the right track for the first time in nearly a decade.

Like the other tools that weaken traceability, presidential/congressional summits are no panacea. Sometimes they fail because neither side wants to compromise, as with the 1987 budget summit, or because there is no immediate pressure to solve the problem, as with the 1988 health care commission (Gilmour 1992, 253). Summits may be able to produce a solution to collective action problems, but the rank-and-file members still must support the overall package. The advantage of this technique is that many of the details of difficult negotiations can be worked out by the leadership, which can take more of the heat if things go wrong.

Fast-track mechanisms on trade packages combine several of the above techniques. Congress delegates authority to a special trade representative to negotiate a trade agreement. The agreement then comes back to Congress under a closed or restrictive rule that prevents the agreement from unraveling. This "take it or leave it" approach allowed Congress to pass the 1979 Trade Act, the 1988 Canadian Free Trade Agreement, the North American Free Trade Agreement (NAFTA), and the General Agreement on Trade and Tariffs (GATT). The collective dilemma is minimized in this instance because members who generally support free trade and would like to support the bill can attempt to pacify constituents who are opposed to specific parts of a trade agreement (such as environmental provisions) by pointing out that there was no opportunity to modify the legislation. However, this approach is no longer in favor on the Hill. In 1998, Congress refused to extend fast-track authority to the Clinton administration, indicating a reluctance to transfer that much power to the executive branch.

While each of these mechanisms, and the two we discuss in more detail below, help overcome the collective dilemma, there are obvious disadvantages as well. The two most important potential problems are a transfer of too much power to other branches and a lack of accountability (Schoenbrod 1993). Balancing the benefits of these procedures against the potential costs is a tricky exercise. An awareness of the danger of delegating too much power to the president must be vigilantly maintained by congressional leaders. In most instances, this is a built-in reflex for Congress. The continual battle over the institutional balance of power ensures that neither branch will gain the upper hand for too long. The other danger of losing collective accountability is less of a problem. All of the mechanisms that we discuss here provide for some accountability. The two that pose the greatest danger are omnibus bills and delegation. But even in these cases, electoral accountability can be imposed on any member who steps too far out of line, or on any party that abuses the tools at its disposal. While the United States does not have a system of responsible party government, the 1994 elections demonstrated that the governing party may be held accountable for perceived abuses of institutional power.

The ultimate goal of weakening the traceability chain is to provide Congress with the ability to act in the nation's collective interests when it needs to, without encouraging irresponsible behavior, blame shifting, or self-interested behavior. The next two mechanisms, bipartisan commissions and greater insulation for Congress, seem especially promising.

Bipartisan Commissions

We noted in Chapter 1 that military base closures presented Congress with a classic collective dilemma, in that no individual member was willing to pay the price for shutting down a base in his or her district, even though there was unanimous agreement that there were too many bases.[4]

In this case—although it took several years for Congress to settle on an effective policy—legislators managed to find a solution. How did they do it? In 1988, Congress created a bipartisan commission, called the Independent Commission on Base Realignment and Closures (BRAC). The Commission was responsible for reviewing existing military bases and recommending which bases should be closed. The Commission forwarded its recommendations to the secretary of defense and the president, who could either approve the entire list or reject it; neither could add or remove bases from the list. The key is that once the list was approved, Congress could only block the closures by voting to reject the entire list. Members, therefore, gave up their ability to protect their pet bases, in the interest of collective efficiency. It worked brilliantly: in the first round of closures, the commission successfully recommended that dozens of installations be closed down.

The process worked so well, in fact, that Congress reauthorized three more rounds of closures (in 1990, 1993, and 1995). By 1998, ninety-seven major bases and hundreds of small installations had been closed, with savings of $14 billion between 1988 and 2001 (U.S. Department of Defense 1998, 64). The genius of the base closing commission idea is that it substituted a reasonably rational process for what had become a legislative free-for-all. It allowed members to accept the local harm of base closures, since they could credibly claim that it was not their doing. Moreover, to use Arnold's term, the "traceability chain" was broken because it was difficult to pin any one vote to a closure act. The Commission was clearly intended to accomplish this objective, as the timing and procedural mechanisms of the entire process were structured to provide political cover for members whose districts would suffer economic harm. As a result, legislators could take credit for the collective benefit, while no one had to pay the political cost of producing it.

One example of how the chain was broken comes from the very act of establishing the commission process. The second, third, and fourth rounds of base closures were authorized in 1990 as an amendment to the fiscal year 1991 defense budget authorization. The amendment was adopted on a voice vote, and because there was no roll call vote, it is impossible to determine how members voted. The next round of closures was slated to begin in 1993, meaning that several years, an election, and one round of redistricting would elapse before any more bases were closed. By then, it would be utterly impossible for constituents to sort out who had supported what. This is a dramatic display of how a lack of immediate accountability can help produce collectively beneficial results.

But delegation has its limits. In 1998, when DoD requested authorization to begin a fifth round of base closures in 2001, Congress balked. Both the House and Senate refused to include language in their defense authorization bills to renew the BRAC process, and on June 25 the Senate narrowly approved (on a 48 to 45 vote) an amendment to the 1999 defense budget bill to make it more difficult for DoD to close bases. Senators expressed concern over the accuracy of DoD data on the cost savings from base closures, and others simply wanted a breather between the first four rounds and any future efforts. But Senator Carl Levin (D–Mich.) had no patience with these arguments, arguing that the provision "tells our soldiers that despite what we say, our real priority would be to protect our turf back home" (*Congressional Record*, June 24, 1998, S6983). Public attentiveness to the issue no doubt has weakened with the drop in the deficit and a sharp decline in defense spending from its apex in 1985. Nevertheless, it is telling that even those who voted to block further closures voiced their support for the BRAC principle.

Insulating Congress

Our next recommendation is bound not to be popular with the public or with groups who strive to create a responsive and open Congress. But in our view, one of the greatest obstacles to responsible policymaking is giving too much access to interested parties who will be adversely affected by the policy changes. It is hard enough for members of Congress to raise taxes on tobacco, get rid of dairy price supports, or abandon various forms of "corporate welfare" without having the affected parties in the room when the decisions are made. In some instances, Congress has been willing to go behind closed doors to make tough choices, as with the 1986 Tax Reform Act. In their memorable account of the passage of the act, *Showdown at Gucci Gulch*, journalists Jeffrey Birnbaum and Alan Murray described how reform started to unravel as the bill was loaded up with billions of dollars of breaks for special interests in what they called "the Gucci Boys revenge." Finance Committee Chair Robert Packwood (R–Ore.) realized that something dramatic had to be done, so he started from scratch by slashing tax rates lower than anyone thought possible, while eliminating many deductions that the lobbyists wanted to preserve. Packwood also realized that such a bold move would have to be carried out in closed session. Birnbaum and Murray describe the high drama that ensued in "Gucci Gulch" (the reference is to the hallway outside the Senate Finance Committee room, where the high-priced lobbyists in their tailored suits and Gucci shoes hang out): "Lobbyists and reporters were massed outside the room, restlessly pacing the corridor's gray marble floors. All they knew was what Packwood had said publicly: that the committee was going to 'start from square one' and that 'nothing is sacred.' The lobbyists were worried, and anxious to find out what was happening inside" (Birnbaum and Murray, 1987, 209). It is clear that the dramatic change in the tax code would not have been possible without throwing the "Gucci boys" out into the hall.

Douglas Arnold argues that members of Congress have generally learned the lesson that the "sunshine laws" have had unintended effects that make lawmaking more difficult:

> Most important, perhaps, is that legislators have been willing to ignore some of the reforms that have not worked. . . . Legislators have discovered the strengths and weaknesses of specific procedures by trial and error. Open meetings, open rules, and unlimited recorded votes seemed like good ideas when they were proposed, and they were backed by Common Cause and others who sought to reduce the power of spe-

cial interests. Unfortunately, these reforms were based on a faulty understanding of the mechanisms that allow for citizens' control. We now know that open meetings filled with lobbyists, and recorded votes on scores of particularistic amendments, serve to increase the powers of special interests, not to diminish them (1990, 275).

However, closed sessions are still relatively rare. Since 1975, Congress has not even kept records on the number of closed committee meetings because "virtually all committee meetings have been open" (Ornstein, Mann, and Malbin 1998, 127); therefore, members have not been willing to apply the lessons of unintended consequences very often. Between 1973 and 1995, a majority of members on a House committee *could* vote to close a meeting, but at the start of the 104th Congress House Republicans imposed a stiffer standard, requiring that all meetings be open "unless it would pose a threat to national security" (Ornstein, Mann, and Malbin 1998, 127).

This standard is far too restrictive. We recommend that Congress return to the pre–sunshine era practice in which about one-third of all committee meetings were closed. A majority of members should be able to close any committee meeting when they believe that the collective interests of the nation would be served. Closing markup sessions where the legislation is discussed and revised would allow members to negotiate without the bright lights of television or the watchful eye of the lobbyist. All committee hearings would still be open (except those involving issues of national security), and recorded committee votes would still be made public and included with published committee reports. In other words, accountability would not be undermined, rather the collective lawmaking capacities of Congress would be improved. As the 1966 Joint Committee on the Organization of Congress final report concluded, "While open hearings should always be encouraged, not all committee *meetings* need to be open to the public. Executive sessions are required for informal discussion and reconciliation of views" (Senate Report 1414 1966, 11).

We strongly concur with Joseph Bessette's assessment that the closed committee meeting would allow Congress to better serve the national interest, or in our terms to overcome the collective dilemma. According to Bessette,

> If national policy ought to be merely the aggregation of the perceived interests of the geographic parts of the nation, then there is no problem [with an open legislative process]. But if there is such a thing as a national interest in areas like defense policy, international trade, domestic economic policy, responsible budgeting, or social welfare that cannot be reduced to the perceived interests of the geographical parts of the nation, then it is the responsibility of those we send to the House and Senate to reason together about how to achieve it. Such collective deliberation will be rendered

impossible if the members of the House and Senate are, like ambassadors from sovereign states, bound down in their day-to-day policymaking efforts to what is acceptable to their geographic constituencies (Bessette 1994, 224).

There is no better example of the *virtues* of at least a little secrecy and insulation from outside forces than how Congress is handling the Clinton-Lewinsky scandal and the impeachment process that has begun. Once Independent Counsel Kenneth Starr transmitted a report to Congress, in which he provided extensive evidence of what he considered impeachable offenses, virtually every document in the investigation was released to the public. Included in these releases is material that would normally remain under seal, particularly transcripts and videotape of grand jury testimony. The House put most of the documents on the World Wide Web, leading to a breathtakingly broad public distribution.

Whatever one thinks of the case against Clinton, there is a wide consensus that Congress has damaged itself in the public's eye by how it has handled the matter. Between September 12 and October 7, 1998, public approval of Congress dropped from 55 percent to 44 percent (CNN/Gallup/USA Today, October 8, 1998), and majorities opposed the release of Clinton's grand jury testimony and the initiation of impeachment hearings. In an October CBS News poll, only 34 percent of the public approved of the way that the House Judiciary Committee was doing its job, against 53 percent who disapproved. When the House voted on December 19, 1998, to impeach Clinton, the president's public approval rating *rose*, from 61 percent to 71 percent in a Pew Center poll. Even among those who voted to impeach the president, there was growing sentiment that the House had acted rashly. Two days after the vote, four Republicans—all of whom had voted to impeach Clinton—released a letter to Senate Majority Leader Trent Lott (R–Miss.) in which they expressed their support for censuring Clinton rather than removing him from office (Bennett and Mitchell 1998, 1). Whether or not the Senate votes to convict Clinton and remove him from office (an unlikely outcome, in our view), there is no doubt that the process has been messy, disputatious, and indecorous.

Contrast this with the public's reaction to how Congress handled Watergate. At the end of that process, public approval of Congress went up by twenty points, and the period is often considered the high-water mark of institutional integrity and constitutional deliberation. Nobody, we surmise, will make the same sort of arguments about the Clinton flap.

One major difference between the two scandals: In 1998, Congress opened the entire process to immediate and widespread public scrutiny, with almost no filtering. In 1974, the process was far more insulated from public view. Although the Senate held televised hearings, most of the House impeachment process was conducted in secret. The House Judiciary Committee began its inquiry in May 1974, but closed the hearings from the public and the media. Although the decision was criticized at the time—journalist Elizabeth Drew wrote that "the leaks, the long time that the committee seems to be taking, and the lack of public understanding of what it is doing has cast a pall over the Committee's deliberations" (Drew 1975, 294)—analyst Norman Ornstein has argued that the secrecy was crucial: "Committee members were more apt to weigh the evidence and less likely to play to the cameras or their constituents. The members also built a consensus that cut across party lines. Only after the committee decided to consider articles of impeachment against Nixon were the deliberations opened to the public, and only then was the evidence and the reasoning behind the committee's judgment aired for citizens to consider" (Ornstein 1998, 27).

The Clinton impeachment process has been so contentious and partisan that the public could doubt its legitimacy. That is a bad position from which to make grave constitutional decisions. The last-minute decision to hold the closing debates of the Senate trial in secret was a deviation from the pattern of excessive openness. However, at that point, the decision was viewed by the public as an unwarranted, undemocratic move, rather than a welcome breather from the "all-Monica, all-the-time" coverage of the previous twelve months. Making important decisions out of the public eye will never be popular, but it is one way to overcome the collective dilemma.

Deliberation in Congress

Casual observers of American politics are often shocked when they see television coverage of debates in the House or Senate in which members make impassioned pleas to empty chambers. More likely than not, there may be only a handful of interested members listening to the debate and a few more milling around in the back. When a roll call vote is taken the floor becomes a beehive of activity for about fifteen minutes and then quickly empties again. As the American Enterprise Institute/Brookings Institution report, *Renewing Congress*, noted, "[T]he quality of debate in Congress has been diminished as members spend less time on the floor and come to votes preprogrammed on issues by information gleaned from staff and lobbyists. There is little real interaction and discussion among members. What passes for debate are often lonely declamations by members or senators at times when legislative business has been concluded" (Mann and Ornstein 1993, 57).

Deliberation *does* occur in the House, but much of it is out of the public eye (Bessette 1994, chapter 6; Smith 1989, 236–46). However, even the behind-the-scenes legislating is neglected by members whose time is so limited. One member who participated in the Brookings Institution session on congressional reform noted the institutional consequences of more deliberation:

> If you started urging or encouraging or forcing members to start devoting time to legislating or going to committees and so on, first of all, they would have less time for all this nonsense of flame throwing or bomb throwing or whatever it is on the floor, and, secondly they might even learn that there is something of interest and usefulness that they can do to get things done. We have so few members who really give very much time (Mann and Ornstein 1992, 31).

Senator Robert Byrd (D–W.Va.), one of the most vigorous defenders of Congress as an institution, notes that deliberation serves an important function for the public and that the Senate needs to try to restore its status as the "world's greatest deliberative body":

> In a representative democracy, the people must face issues and understand them before elected officials can responsibly act to put into effect acceptable and workable solutions. . . . In our system, the Senate's role as a deliberative body should be to endeavor to help the people hear all sides so that consensus may form; yet, as an institution the Senate is more and more ceasing to perform that deliberative function. It is not the Senate that I once knew. The Senate has lost its soul. . . . I am not sure that the Senators of today clearly perceive time spent on the Senate floor, debating the issues of the day, as the best way in which to use their always-limited time. Senate debate is dying as a legislative art. I believe that the Congress is held in low esteem today partially because of this. Any more, one hears little Senate floor discussion of the great issues of the day. Too often, to the casual observer, Congress must seem somehow disconnected, irrelevant, distracted, and self-absorbed (Senate Hearing 103–26 1993, 5–6).

Byrd's observation that deliberation in Congress can help form public consensus echoes the famous argument by James Madison about one of the central differences between a democracy and a republic. In a republic, people delegate decisionmaking powers to elected representatives rather than maintaining the direct power to govern, as would be true in a democracy. Madison argued that a republic will "refine and enlarge the public views, by passing them through the medium of a chosen body of citizens. . . . Under such a regulation, it may well happen that the public voice, will be more consonant to the public good than if pronounced by the people themselves, convened for that purpose" (*Federalist* 10).[5]

Madison was arguing that the public will not always be served by a responsive Congress. Indeed, as undemocratic as it may sound, Congress should not always follow public opinion. Just because a majority of the public supports a given issue does not mean that it is good policy, as the examples, we would argue, of term limits, the balanced budget amendment, school prayer, and flag burning demonstrate. Similarly, just because a majority of the public *does not* support a given policy doesn't mean that it isn't a good idea. For example, the Marshall Plan, the massive effort by the United States to help rebuild Western Europe after World War II, was opposed by large majorities of the public, yet it was clearly the right thing to do. Foreign aid in general is not popular with the public, but the United States cannot cut itself off from the rest of the world. Stated more formally, public opinion is neither a necessary nor a sufficient condition for good public policy.[6]

Unfortunately, it is not possible to *force* members of Congress to engage in meaningful debates. However, we believe that if the opportunity for a more deliberative process is presented, members will take advantage of it. The survey taken of members in 1993 that was cited in Chapter 3 indicated that nearly 60 percent of members said they would like to spend more time attending floor debate or watching in on television. About half of those listed it as one of their two top priorities of how they would like to spend additional time. Of the twelve activities asked about, participating more in debates ranked second in terms of how members would like to spend more time (spending more time studying and reading about legislation was the top-ranked item) (U.S. Congress 1993, 275–280).

Two of the reforms we proposed above should provide more opportunity for deliberation. Closed committee meetings will help encourage more discussion in committee. While we recognize Senator Byrd's point that *public* deliberation is important to help build public consensus on issues, this must be balanced against the need for Congress to insulate itself from lobbyists. Public hearings in committees, closed committee markups when necessary, and then open and vigorous debate on the floor will achieve the best balance between the competing goals of responsiveness and responsibility. Our proposed campaign finance reforms would also help free up members to spend more time deliberating.

Finally, we recommend holding a series of Oxford-style debates on the floor of the House and the Senate at least once a week. Each side of the debate would have two or three members who would present their views on topics such as crime, welfare, Social Security reform, race relations, and education policy, which would in turn be rebutted and critiqued by the opposing side. Some time could be reserved for a more general participation from the broader group of members. This forum would help serve the public education function that is discussed in more detail below, provide a forum for members' ideas, and help restore confidence in the institution. Members support the idea of Oxford-style debates, with 43 percent of the 155 members who answered the survey saying they "strongly favored" the debates on "major issues of the day," while 30 percent were opposed (the remainder were equally in favor and opposed) (U.S. Congress 1993, 272).[7] The *Renewing Congress* report concluded, "The country needs and wants focused and organized discussion of this sort as it moves to the 21st century. Congress needs to show that is it grappling with key problems and debating real alternatives. And the country will undoubtedly develop a different impression of Congress once it sees the serious men and women who are there dealing with real and important issues" (Mann and Ornstein 1992, 51).

Before the onset of the Persian Gulf War, the Senate engaged in a "debate" on whether or not we should have a war. While this was not really a debate, but rather a series of personal and impassioned speeches, the nation was captivated and the discussion served an important purpose.

Public Education

It is ironic that as Congress has, by most measures, become a more open and democratically responsive organization, public opinion believes that members pay less and less attention to what their constituents think. The percentage of respondents in the National Election Study who say that most members pay little attention to what their constituents think rose from 16 percent in 1964 to 25 percent in 1980. The number who say that members pay a "good deal" of attention to their constituents dropped dramatically, from 44 percent in 1964 to 17 percent in 1980. Although the NES has stopped asking this precise question, so there is no more recent data, it is a safe bet that these numbers have dropped even further. General cynicism and apathy are reflected in the extent to which the public ignores Congress. More than half of the public does not know which party controls Congress, and about three-quarters typically cannot name their representative. As the "Public Accountability Project" concluded:

> The success of self-government depends in large measure on informed citizen participation. Members of Congress believe a growing number of Americans are distressingly uninformed about the ways Congress and government work, inattentive to political news and developments, and disinterested in available opportunities to interact, communicate with, and influence elected officials (U.S. Congress 1993, 185).

Members of Congress see this as one of the most important problems facing the institution. In the 1993 survey, 56 percent of members cited the "public's understanding of Congress" as one of the five most important issues facing the institution (out of the eight issues, it was mentioned with the fourth greatest frequency), and 84 percent of members "strongly agreed" that it was a problem, while only 3 percent "strongly disagreed" that it was a problem (U.S. Congress 1993, 251, 257).

The lack of citizen participation and interest occurs despite the best efforts of a broad range of institutions. The Robert A. Taft Institute of Government, the Close Up Foundation, the American Political Science Association's Congressional Fellows Program, the U.S. House and Senate Historical Offices, the Dirksen Congressional Leadership Research Center, and the Carl Albert Center all have extensive outreach and education programs for various constituencies, ranging from high school students and teachers, political scientists and journalists, to the general public. All of these institutions share the goal of increasing the public's understanding of Congress. However, these efforts clearly are not enough.

Other recent developments should also help. One is the movement known as "civic journalism," in which television and radio stations and newspapers have banded together to bring the public back into the political process. By holding town meetings and forums on broad ranges of issues, and then reporting on the results in the media outlets, the civic journalism project is clearly a step in the right direction. Another important development is the explosion of information on the Internet. While at the end of the 1990s this resource is only utilized by a minority of the country (about 30 percent), exit polls from the 1996 presidential election showed that 10 percent of the electorate said that they used information from the Internet to help them decide how to vote. Some of the popular news sites, such as the now defunct "Politics Now" site, were receiving 1.5 million hits a day at the peak of the election campaign. Some Congress-specific sites can also arm voters with valuable information about their representatives. Vote Smart's "Congress Track" project provides information on all members' voting records, while the Library of Congress's "Thomas" site and the Government Printing Office's "GPO Access" site are comprehensive sources of information about current activities in Congress.

The burden of the public education efforts will fall on members of Congress, journalists who cover Congress, and educators who study the institution and American politics more generally. Leaders need to play more of a role in informing the public about the nature of Congress's agenda. While this cuts against the grain of the incentives of modern campaigning, we think members should try to explain to their constituents the complexities of the legislative process rather than simply pretending that complex issues have simple solutions. Journalists should also aid in this process of education. Rather than focusing so much attention on the negative aspects of national politics, the media would better serve the public by intelligent, issue-based coverage. Congress can aid in this effort by creating an Institutional Communication Office that would provide nonpartisan information on the operations of Congress, including "important events in congressional history, statistics and precedents, and historical comparisons" (Hess 1994, 152). This proposal comes from Stephen Hess, who notes, "Because institutional reporting does not come comfortably to the mainstream American press, Congress must be better prepared to help explain–and defend—itself (Hess 1994, 153). The model that we have in mind is something like the Congressional Budget Office (CBO) for general information on Congress. The CBO has an excellent reputation for providing timely, accurate information on the economy and the budget. The Institutional Communication Office could provide a similar service to journalists, educators, and citizens who want reliable, accurate information on Congress.

Conclusion

Any reform effort is open to the criticism that, since change must occur *within* the legislature itself, there is no way that members will agree as long as they can benefit from the existing circumstances (indeed, some of the reforms enacted in the most recent effort—in 1995—have failed). Also, as we note above, no organizational reforms will provide the silver bullet that will solve every institutional ailment. Nevertheless, we have suggested a range of reforms that should appeal to the individual incentives of members of Congress (such as closing committee meetings, providing more party money for campaigns, and helping repair Congress's image with the public). At the same time, we recognize that in the end, the effectiveness of reforms rests with the voting public. The ultimate authority and accountability in a representative democracy resides in the voting booth. If citizens do not put pressure on representatives to change the political process by removing those who resist change, Congress will not change. Without electoral accountability, nothing else matters.

Despite the discussion of disaffection, cynicism, and need for reform, one should not lose sight of the fact that Congress has actually served the public interest remarkably well for over 200 years. The institution deserves respect for its ability to govern over two centuries, in a variety of trying and difficult circumstances, while balancing the difficult aims of geographic responsiveness and collective accountability.

The theme of this book has been that there are no permanent solutions to the collective dilemma. The legislative process is a messy balancing of national, district, partisan, and ideological interests. Therefore, Congress is not dysfunctional; it's just that representation is hard.

Discussion Questions

Chapter 1

1. Do you think that elected representatives should act primarily according to what their constituents want (as delegates) or according to what they themselves think is in the national interest (as trustees)? When the two roles conflict, how should members decide how to act?

2. Do you think that "rational choice" explanations accurately describe the way that individuals make decisions? Can you identify different contexts in which rational choice theory would be especially applicable? In what contexts would it be especially inapplicable?

3. Do you approve or disapprove of the way that Congress is currently handling its job? Why? Do you approve or disapprove of the way that *your representative or senator* is handling his or her job? Is there a difference in your two answers?

Chapter 2

1. What would the Framers (Madison, Hamilton, and so forth) think of the contemporary Congress?

2. How has the job of being a representative or senator changed over the years?

3. In what ways do the contemporary and historical Congresses differ? In what ways are they similar?

Chapter 3

1. In the first part of the chapter we argued that the examples of the tobacco legislation and the Clinton health care plan demonstrate the various complexities of the collective dilemma. What are the arguments supporting the contention that these two cases demonstrate that Congress supports the narrow, special interests over the public good? What are the arguments that the public good may have been served (or considered) as well?

2. Trace out the dimensions of the policy and institutional dilemmas for the health care and tobacco cases. How are they similar and how do they differ?

3. How are the conditions that promote the collective dilemma worse at the end of the 1990s than they were in the 1970s? To what extent are things not that different?

4. How does the example of campaign finance reform illustrate the collective dilemma?

Chapter 4

1. What are the basic goals of congressional reform and what are the tradeoffs among those goals?

2. Which goals of reform would you emphasize if you were chairing a committee on congressional reform?

3. How one answers the previous question depends in part on one's view of the proper representational role of members of Congress. Should Congress descriptively represent our nation; that is, should they "look like us"? Do you favor the trustee or delegate model of representation? How does your position on the proper representational role for a member of Congress affect your views on reform?

4. Which of the reforms of the 1970s and 1990s strengthened the collective decision-making capacity of Congress? Which of them weakened that capacity? Which of these reforms do you favor and why?

5. Which of the proposed congressional reforms that we criticize do you find attractive and why? Do any of these reforms address the underlying problem of the collective dilemma? Why or why not?

6. What are the cycles of congressional reform? Where are we in the cycle at this moment? What does this mean for the next round of reforms?

Chapter 5

1. How likely is major congressional reform to occur in the next few years? What would make reform more likely, or less likely?

2. Richard Schoenbrod, a Yale law professor, criticizes congressional delegation to executive branch agencies as creating unaccountable and undemocratic policymaking institutions. How would this apply to our proposal to make use of bipartisan commissions?

3. What are the advantages and disadvantages of allowing Congress to make some decisions behind closed doors?

4. Which of the reforms that we recommend do you think would address the collective dilemma? Are there other reforms that you would suggest?

5. How would your answers to questions 3 and 4 change if the majority party in Congress changed?

Glossary

Bicameral legislative system or bicameralism   A system in which legislative authority is divided between two chambers, with different members, terms, and electoral constituencies. Splitting authority into separate units makes enacting legislation more difficult, since lawmaking requires the agreement of two institutions rather than one. At the same time, it can encourage deliberation and compromise.

Bipartisan commissions   Committees or groups, composed of members of both political parties, charged with devising policies or legislation considered too controversial for Congress to handle effectively. By including both parties, these commissions often avoid the charge that they are acting in the political interest of one party. A recent example is the Base Realignment and Closure Commission, which identified military bases for elimination.

Candidate-centered politics   *See* Politician-centered politics.

Casework   The practice, among legislators, of resolving problems that their constituents are having with the government. Usually, casework involves a member investigating a complaint against an agency (a delayed Social Security check, denial of benefits, a contract awarded to a competitor), obtaining an explanation of the agency's action, and persuading the agency to address the constituent's concerns, where warranted.

Christmas tree bill   A bill that is sure to pass, because it is so popular that few would dare oppose it. In these cases, members often attempt to add amendments (or riders) to the bill in the hope that the amendments will sail through with little notice.

Cloture   The method of ending debate in the Senate, in response to a filibuster. According to Senate rules, if sixty senators vote to end debate, further deliberations are limited an additional thirty hours. After this time elapses, there is a vote on the measure under consideration. If the supporters of a bill fail to get sixty votes to end debate, they usually withdraw the legislation.

Collective dilemma   A situation that occurs when individually rational behavior produces a collective outcome that none of the individuals would have preferred. The "dilemma" arises because individually rational behavior results in collectively irrational outcomes. *See also* Prisoner's dilemma; Tragedy of the commons.

Committee markup sessions   The point during which congressional committees revise legislation, after committee hearings are held. At markup sessions, members propose amendments to the bill, with committee members voting to approve or reject the recommendations. At the end of the markup session, the full committee votes on whether to report the "perfected" bill to the chamber floor.

Committee of the Whole   For parliamentary reasons, the House often convenes as the "Committee of the Whole House on the State of the Union." The Committee of the

Whole acts as a committee made up of all representatives. The Committee of the Whole operates under less restrictive procedural rules than the House: 100 members constitute a quorum, instead of the 218 required for the House; time limits for debate on amendments are five minutes (rather than an hour in the House); 25 members may request a recorded vote, instead of 218; and a motion to end debate does not immediately cut off consideration of all further amendments.

Constituency service   The practice of performing casework or providing other benefits (such as pork barrel spending) for one's geographic constituency.

Continental Congress   The first form of government that emerged during the American Revolution, and which was formalized by the Articles of Confederation, adopted in 1781. The Continental Congress was a unicameral legislature that exercised both legislative and executive functions. In the Congress, each state delegation had a single vote, and the states retained control over many critical functions, including the power to make foreign policy, levy taxes, and raise armies. Inefficiency and a lack of sufficient power crippled the Continental Congress, and concern over its inability to govern led to the Constitutional Convention in 1787.

Contract with America   The legislative agenda promoted by Representative Newt Gingrich (R–Ga.) before the 1994 midterm election. The contract promised that within 100 days of a G.O.P.-led Congress, Republicans would vote on a variety of legislative and policy reforms. These included, among other things, deregulation, welfare reform, a balanced budget constitutional amendment, term limits, and tax reform. The Contract is widely viewed as one key to the Republicans obtaining a majority in both the House and Senate in the midterm election.

Cumulative voting   A scheme in which voters are granted more than one vote, which they can distribute among candidates (or legislative alternatives), or concentrate on one alternative. In elections for four legislative districts, for example, voters would have four votes that they could distribute in any way they chose. Cumulative voting is designed to enhance minority representation, by taking the intensity of preferences into account.

Delegate model of representation   According to this model, the proper role of a legislator is to mirror constituency opinion at all times, even if doing so conflicts with what the member thinks is in the district's interests. Members acting as delegates vote according to what the constituency wants. The alternative is the trustee model.

Demosclerosis   A popular term describing Congress's inability to act, caused by excessive openness to public demands.

Descriptive representation   Representing a constituency based on the demographic characteristics of that constituency. Descriptive representation is usually considered in the context of how well a representative body reflects the racial or gender composition of the population.

Direct mail   The practice of sending political or commercial mail to targeted populations. By creating mailing lists of people with special characteristics (e.g., registered Republicans, people who have given money to environmental groups in the past, homeowners, subscribers to *New Republic*), fund-raisers and organizers can more easily identify and reach those individuals most likely to respond to solicitations. Direct mail techniques, which became widespread in the 1980s, dramatically increased the ability of political organizations to raise money and mobilize supporters.

Disappearing quorum   A tactic used in the latter half of the nineteenth century to delay legislation in the House. When a member raised a point of order that a quorum was not present, members of the opposition party, although present on the floor, would refuse to answer the roll call. In this way, even though a quorum was actually present, the rules would not allow a formal recognition of the fact.

Distributive policies   Those policies which provide localized and divisible benefits to identifiable constituencies. Military spending, agricultural subsidies, and highway construction funds are classic examples of distributive policies.

Electronic town hall   An increasingly popular mechanism for public control of policy, advocated by H. Ross Perot, among others. The idea behind the electronic town hall is to submit proposals to the public, organized into small groups across the nation. Using computer and telecommunications technology, the town hall groups would cast their votes to a centralized location for instant tabulation.

The Federalist Papers   A series of newspaper editorials, written by James Madison, Alexander Hamilton, and John Jay under the pseudonym Publius, which argued in support of the proposed Constitution. These essays are considered the most important statements about the political theory underlying the constitutional structure of American government.

Federalists   Supporters of the proposed Constitution were known as Federalists, while those opposed were known as Anti-Federalists. In the 1790s, the Federalists emerged as the precursors of the first political parties, with members generally supportive of a strong central government.

Filibuster   A method of halting all legislative deliberations in the Senate. According to Senate rules, there is no limit on how long members may speak, and senators can threaten to stall indefinitely by talking for extended periods, and by using other parliamentary procedures. The threat of a filibuster, especially at the end of a legislative session when there is great pressure to consider legislation in a short time, can force sponsors to drop their bills or force compromises. Senators can cut off debate by invoking cloture, which requires sixty votes. *See* Cloture.

The Framers   The individuals who wrote the Constitution and other founding documents of American government. Prominent Framers include James Madison, Alexander Hamilton, Thomas Jefferson, and George Washington.

Free rider   A problem that arises in the production of public goods. Since anyone can enjoy a public good once it is produced, there is no incentive to pay the costs of producing that good. As a result, everyone has an incentive to free ride by receiving the benefits, but not to pay the costs. With respect to the institutional dilemma, free riders enjoy the consequences produced by legislators who tend to the organizational needs of Congress, even as they refuse to participate in these institutional maintenance activities.

Geographic representation   A method of representation in which discrete geographic units (congressional districts, states) select legislators to represent them. Under this system, legislators have divided incentives, and must represent local interests as well as the "national" interest. One result is "parochialism," or the tendency to view policy in terms of its effect on one's constituency.

Grassroots lobbying   Organizing political activity at the mass level, involving "common folk" instead of high-level political operatives. The objective of a grassroots campaign is to mobilize a large group of the public to make their preferences clear. A more recent practice is to create the false impression of a mass-based political movement, which is in fact maintained by well-financed and organized interests (often called "astroturf lobbying").

Gridlock   An inability to enact legislation, usually the result of divided government and failure to achieve agreement between the president and Congress.

Imperial presidency   In the early 1970s, Arthur Schlesinger Jr. argued that the presidency had become too powerful, especially in foreign affairs. Johnson and Nixon's prosecution of the Vietnam War in the face of growing congressional opposition, and the Watergate scandal, raised questions about how well constitutional and statutory limits could constrain the president. One result of this era was the War Powers Act, a law which attempted to limit the president's ability to commit U.S. troops to foreign conflicts.

Incumbency advantage   The electoral edge that incumbents have over challengers. Incumbents almost always enjoy higher name recognition and fund-raising ability than challengers, a difference which is reflected in the high re-election rate for incumbents (especially in the House). In the second half of the twentieth century, more than 90 percent of House incumbents and 80 percent of Senate incumbents who ran for re-election won.

Institutional dilemma   A situation in which legislators who rationally act in their own self-interest hurt the legislature as a whole. Two examples are members criticizing Congress publicly (helping their own re-election efforts, but diminishing the public stature of Congress) and members spending time on campaign tasks at the expense of their legislative duties.

Institutional maintenance   The task of looking after the institutional needs of Congress, by performing key organizational and administrative functions. Historically, party leadership and key committees (especially Rules and Appropriations) have performed this job.

Institutional norms   Expectations about how members of the House and Senate will behave, distinguished from formal rules. The most important norms have historically been deference to committees, civility in debate, courtesy to other members, reciprocity, apprenticeship, and specialization. There is general agreement that these norms have weakened in recent decades.

Joint Committee on the Organization of Congress   A committee created in 1992 to study congressional organization and recommend reforms. The committee report, released in December 1993, suggested some minor changes, but its impact was overshadowed by the Republican victory in the 1994 midterm election.

Judicial review   The power of the courts to declare acts of Congress and the executive branch unconstitutional.

King of the Hill procedure A special rule that stipulates that in a sequential voting procedure on different versions of a bill, the last version to be adopted by a majority vote is the one that stands. One other version of this procedure stipulates that the version that gets the most votes is the one that wins.

Legislative Reform Act of 1946 The first postwar congressional reform, enacted in response to concerns that Congress had grown weak in comparison to the presidency. The Act reduced the number of committees by more than half, reorganized committee jurisdictions, provided for professional staff, raised member salaries, and required registration of lobbyists.

Line item veto According to constitutional doctrine, presidents may veto or approve entire bills; they may not selectively veto some parts of a bill and approve others. A line item veto would give the president this authority, which many state governors have. In 1996, Congress passed the Line Item Veto Act, allowing the president to strike out certain types of spending and tax provisions in legislation presented to him. In 1998, however, the Supreme Court rejected this practice as unconstitutional.

Lobbies/interest groups Organizations formed to persuade Congress to support specific policies or legislative positions.

Logrolling The practice of members cooperating with each other, usually by one member exchanging his or her support for another member's bill for that member's support of his or her own bill. William Safire, in his *Political Dictionary*, notes the classic statement of logrolling by one of Lincoln's cabinet secretaries: "you scratch my back, and I'll scratch yours."

Omnibus legislation Large bills that package together a variety of smaller pieces of legislation. The package must be voted on in a single up or down vote and cannot be separated into parts.

Open rules *See* Restrictive rules.

Oxford-style debates One of the proposed reforms that would enhance Congress's deliberative capacity. Debates would follow a structured format in which Democrats and Republicans would present opposing views on the central issues under consideration in Congress on a monthly or biweekly basis.

Parochialism *See* Geographic representation.

Party leadership The group of people within the Democratic and Republican parties in the House and Senate who have responsibility for helping shape the parties' legislative agendas, scheduling legislation, disseminating information, building coalitions, and controlling debate. The top positions in the House are the Speaker and minority leaders; the Senate leaders are the majority and minority leaders.

Policy dilemma Members often face a tension between doing what is best for the constituents from their home state and what would be best for the entire nation. In some instances this policy dilemma can ultimately damage Congress as an institution, if citizens perceive that Congress is only responsive to geographic constituencies and is unable to tackle the nation's broader problems.

Political action committees (PACs) The political arm of interest groups that collects money from their members and makes contributions to candidates and political parties.

Politician-centered politics   The tendency for candidates and elected officials to be relatively independent of political parties. Candidates usually decide to run for office on their own, raise their own money and conduct their own campaigns, and navigate the legislative process with little interference from political parties.

Pork barrel spending (or "pork")   Programs and policies that provide concentrated benefits for some narrow group or geographic constituency, such as road construction or military bases.

Prisoner's dilemma   Another of the types of collective dilemmas, in which each person acting in his or her own self-interest produces a collective outcome that is not preferred by any of the participants. In this instance, two suspects are separately interrogated by the police. If neither confesses, both will go free. If one confesses, but the other does not, the person who talks will get a lighter sentence than the one who does not. If both confess, they will get an intermediate sentence. Given the circumstances, it is rational for both suspects to confess, even if their preferred outcome, obviously, would be to go free.

Proportional representation   An electoral system in which parties are allocated seats in a representative body in proportion to the percentage of votes that they receive. This form of election encourages third parties because they do not have to win the most votes to obtain some representation.

Proxy voting   The practice whereby congressional committee leaders were able to cast votes for committee members from their party who were absent. Proxy voting gave a tremendous amount of power to committee chairs, who were often able to vote down five or six members from the minority party by themselves. This practice was abolished in 1995.

Public good   A term used in two very different senses that should not be confused. The first is the technical economic definition, which refers to a collective good characterized by indivisibility and nonrival consumption. That is, once the good is provided, it cannot be divided up and sold in smaller parts, and one person's consumption of the good does not diminish another's ability to benefit from the good. The classic example is national defense, which is provided to all citizens. The second sense, and the one used throughout this book, is a policy that is generally good for the entire nation rather than a specific subset of people. The latter is typically referred to as the public good, whereas *the* former is referred to as *a* public good.

Quorum   In Congress, the minimum number of members who must be present to conduct legislative business. In the House, a quorum is 218 members; in the Committee of the Whole, 100; in the Senate, 51. A legislator may raise a point of order that a quorum is not present, which results in a "quorum call" that summons members to the floor. *See also* Disappearing quorum.

Rational actor theory   *See* rational choice theory.

Rational choice theory   This approach to studying politics is rooted in economic models of rational calculation. The theory assumes that individuals are rational actors who have stable preferences and the ability to make decisions based on a ranking of options that produces optimal choices. Strong versions of rational choice theory assume complete information and self-interest, while other variations assume incomplete information and general goal-directed behavior (rather than self-interest).

Republican government   The form of government in which elected representatives govern on behalf of their constituents, as distinguished from direct democracy or monarchy.

Republican revolution   The takeover of Congress by the Republicans in 1994 and the subsequent set of policies and institutional reforms that they attempted to implement.

Responsibility   The notion that members of Congress will act in the collective, long-term interest of the nation, rather than in the short-term, narrow interests of their geographic constituencies. This idea is related to the trustee notion of representation (see below) and requires an institution with strong, centralized legislative capacity.

Responsiveness   When Congress acts in the immediate interests of its constituents and generally tries to reflect public opinion. In general, a responsive institution is decentralized and tends to be more concerned with process than output.

Restrictive rules   When legislation comes to the floor of the House for consideration, a rule must be approved that governs the time and nature of debate over the bill. Restrictive, or closed, rules prevent amendments from being attached to the bill. Open rules allow germane amendments, while modified rules allow some amendments but not others.

Sedition Act   Passed in 1798, this Act was one of four passed to protect the United States from various outside threats (for example, one of the other acts gave the president the power to deport dangerous aliens). The Sedition Act was a crass attempt to silence the critics of the Adams administration. The law outlawed slandering the government, the Congress, or the president (punishable by a $5,000 fine and imprisonment for up to five years). Reaction against these laws contributed to the election of the Jeffersonian Republicans in 1800.

Select committees   Committees that are appointed to examine a specific issue for a relatively short period of time (as opposed to the permanent standing committees that are appointed in each Congress within broader policy jurisdictions). In the early history of Congress, select committees were appointed for every piece of legislation and then disbanded when they reported a bill.

Selective incentives   Inducements provided to actors to help overcome the collective action problem. For example, public radio and public television stations provide coffee mugs or T-shirts to contributors and interest groups provide calendars or group discounts on life insurance as an added incentive to get people to join. Without the selective incentive, more people would be likely to "free ride."

Separation of powers   The U.S. system of government, in which power is divided within and across levels of government. Within each level the legislative, executive, and judicial branches check each other's power. National, state, and local levels of government have separate jurisdiction over different types of policies and share control over others, which means that power is dispersed quite broadly within the U.S. system.

Single-member winner-take-all elections   This form of electoral system is used in the United States for most elections. Single-member districts have one elected official for a specific geographic region. Winner-take-all refers to the practice of allocating all the representation for a given seat to the party that wins the most votes (as opposed to the proportional representation system outlined above). This type of electoral arrangement typically produces a two-party system, because third parties have a difficult time attracting a plurality of the votes, and therefore cannot gain representation in the representative bodies.

Slating organization   An organization that attempts to recruit candidates to run for office and then limits competition against the organization's choice by discouraging others from entering the race.

Soft money   As originally intended by the law, this was money that is contributed to political parties for "party building activities" such as voter education programs and get-out-the-vote drives. These contributions are not subjected to the same limitations as "hard money" contributions that go directly to candidates or are used to advocate the election of a specific candidate. However, loopholes in the law have permitted parties to raise huge sums of money to support national ad campaigns. These ads are legal as long as they do not explicitly urge the election of a specific candidate.

Subcommittee bill of rights   Passed in 1973, this reform guaranteed fixed jurisdictions and adequate staff resources for subcommittees and required committee chairs to refer legislation to the appropriate subcommittee within two weeks (rather than killing legislation by sitting on it).

Substantive representation   Responsive of elected leaders to the policy interests of their constituents. This type of representation may occur with respect to narrow geographic constituencies, or the broader general public.

Sunshine laws   A set of reforms adopted in the 1970s that opened up the political process and provided for more accountability. These reforms included changes in internal rules of Congress that abolished most closed committee meetings and provided for more recorded votes on the floor of the House and Senate and the 1977 Sunshine Act, which required public meetings for about fifty government agencies, regulatory commissions, and advisory committees. Many of these provisions were strengthened further in 1995.

Tariffs   Taxes levied on imported or exported goods. This was the main source of revenue for the federal government in the nineteenth century.

Term limits   Limitations placed on the number of terms that legislators can serve in office. Many states have adopted term limits, but the Supreme Court has ruled that term limits on members of Congress are unconstitutional.

Traceability   The extent to which constituents can easily trace the sources of costs that are imposed on them by legislation passed by Congress.

Tragedy of the commons   When each person acting in his or her self-interest produces a collective outcome that is desired by no one. The specific commons problem arises when each individual farmer grazes as many sheep as possible in the commons area. If each farmer acts this way, the grazing area will be ruined for everyone. The basic logic of the tragedy of the commons is the same as the logic of the collective dilemma and the prisoner's dilemma, outlined above.

Trustee model of representation   When an elected official attempts to enact policies that he or she believes would be in the best interests of his or her constituents, rather than simply giving the people what they want. For example, voters may not want a tax increase, but that may be the best policy to preserve the long-term economic health of the nation given a certain set of conditions.

Utility maximization   Within rational choice theory, the idea that actors will attempt to maximize the net benefits that will be produced by a given decision.

Notes

Introduction

1. The account is drawn from Skeen (1986). The public reaction to the 1816 raise was actually harsher than it was in 1990, as nearly two-thirds of the House membership was newly elected in 1816, against 10 percent turnover in 1990 (Born 1990, 1223; Ornstein, Mann, and Malbin 1998, 61).

2. In Chapter 1 we explore the possibility that some legislators might have a rational interest in reducing the prestige and legitimacy of the institution, if doing so would make it harder for Congress to act. Someone who favored sharply reduced government activism might indeed argue that reducing the institutional capacity of Congress to legislate is a decidedly rational goal. Also, undermining Congress's institutional legitimacy served the short-term partisan goals of the Republicans in the late 1980s and early 1990s as they positioned themselves to become the new majority party in Congress.

3. Political scientist Robert Dahl speaks of the "Madisonian" theory of democracy as "an effort to bring off a compromise between the power of majorities and the power of minorities, between the political equality of all adult citizens on the one side, and the desire to limit their sovereignty on the other" (1956, 4).

4. Yet even the bicameral system does not maximize representation: by giving each state two senators, rather than apportioning Senate seats by population, the Framers sacrificed some measure of representativeness in order to balance competing interests.

Chapter 1

1. A correlation is a measure of the strength of the relationship between two variables that ranges from -1 to 1. The closer the correlation is to 1, the stronger the positive relationship is (as one variable gets bigger, the other gets bigger as well); the closer it is to -1, the stronger the negative relationship is (as one gets bigger, the other gets smaller); and the closer it is to 0, the weaker the relationship is between the two variables. Obviously, these data by themselves say nothing about the direction of causality (or which set of opinions is influencing the other). However, we think it is plausible that general attitudes about the state of the country are more likely to influence attitudes toward Congress than vice versa.

2. Economists use the term *pareto-optimal* to describe this outcome. Pareto-optimality occurs when "it is not possible to improve the well-being of one individual without harming at least one other" (Sandler 1992, 13).

3. Police often use an analogous tactic to take advantage of these incentives by offering leniency for the *first* person to talk in a criminal investigation. Nevertheless, many people

have difficulty accepting this reasoning, arguing that trust, loyalty, or fear of retribution will provide enough incentive so that both individuals keep quiet. It has been shown, moreover, that when the prisoner's dilemma game is repeated indefinitely, players can develop a cooperative strategy that makes both players better off in the long run (Axelrod 1984). If the game is limited to a single iteration, in which both players limit their concern to their immediate self-interest as expressed in the payoff structure, the equilibrium outcome is always for both players to talk. And, we note that the payoff structure is the same for the prisoner's dilemma as it is for the tragedy of the commons (substituting, of course, the choices of overgrazing or not overgrazing for the keep quiet/talk alternatives).

4. This classification is Fenno's (1973, chapter 1). Note that the first two goals clearly relate to *individual* interests, whereas the third has to do with collective interests. We ignore the possibility that members might be interested in securing monetary gains through corruption or other illicit means (Fenno makes this same assumption, 1973, 1).

Chapter 2

1. Much of this discussion was stimulated by Bianco, Spence, and Wilkerson (1996). Although Bianco et al. find evidence of an electoral connection in the early nineteenth century, they also note many differences in institutionalization, career paths, and the logistics of the early Congresses.

2. Our argument does not apply to legislative organizations that are not structured around geographic representation and periodic elections, such as the British House of Lords. Membership in the House of Lords is accorded to members of the British peerage (or people holding the titles of Duke, Earl, Countess, Baron, Lady, and so forth) and certain officials of the Church of England. These members are not elected, and do not represent geographic constituencies. The House of Lords has limited powers, and it is possible to enact a law without its approval.

3. Organized lobbies did exist in England, however, predating Congress by at least one hundred years. These groups arose in response to the same pressures and stimuli that have produced contemporary interest groups: government involvement in more social and economic domains motivated group formation to protect gains once achieved. A group of London merchants who imported tobacco from the American colonies organized a formal association in the mid-1600s to pressure Parliament not to raise import duties. By 1670, they were "so well organized that they not only appeared at the doors of Parliament but also hired counsel to testify on their behalf" (Olson 1983, 364).

4. *Letter to the Electors of England* (1809, 4) .

5. In contrast, in Great Britain the laws governing bribery are ambiguous. It probably is not illegal to offer a bribe to a member of Parliament (M.P.), nor for an M.P to accept one, although this certainly would violate the internal rules of the legislature and subject the member to disciplinary sanctions. Members of Parliament routinely accept retainers from individuals, corporations, and interest groups, and the House of Commons was rocked by scandal in the early 1990s when M.P.s were discovered to be taking money in return for asking specific questions of the Prime Minister during "Question Time" (a weekly session

in which the Prime Minister must appear before the House and answer questions from M.P.s) (Oliver 1997, 125–129).

6. At the same time, many members also described Congress in positive terms. From John Rutledge Jr. (South Carolina), May 29, 1800: "As discontent is inseparable from our nature, it seems impossible for everybody to be satisfied with any set of statesmen, or any kind of policy they may pursue; but the administration of the federal government displays, in my opinion, so much wisdom, integrity, and honor, that I feel confident it will receive from a very large majority of our fellow citizens of these united districts, their deserved approbation" (Cunningham 1978, Vol. I, 223).

Chapter 3

1. Data in *Los Angeles Times* Poll #334 (April 1994). Only 5 percent of respondents said the health care system was "basically sound," and 3 percent were undecided.

2. The most comprehensive effort at explaining the failure of Clinton's Health Security Act is Skocpol (1996). Skocpol traces the demise to fundamental changes in the U.S. political landscape that made it harder to promote *any* major government program: the proliferation of interest groups, electoral demobilization, and a broad effort among conservatives to scale back government.

3. One particularly damaging attack was published by Elizabeth McCaughey-Ross in *The New Republic*, in which she claimed, erroneously, that people would face prison terms for purchasing additional medical services above what the Health Security Act authorized. Despite the inaccuracies, Fallows points out, the claims quickly disseminated into mainstream media coverage of "doctors in jail" (Fallows 1995, 36).

4. But consider this argument: "The fact that a majority supports the goal of universal health insurance is irrelevant. Majorities also desire a balanced budget, would like to eliminate the Castro regime, and so on. The question is whether majorities support means to attractive ends and whether those means are in fact plausible." (White 1995, 379).

5. Newt Gingrich (R–Ga.) was the House minority leader, and became Speaker of the House when the Republicans gained a majority in the 1994 midterm elections. Richard Armey (R–Tex.) was House minority whip, and became majority leader. William Kristol is a Republican strategist, who devised the "no crisis" strategy.

6. However, party organizations and efforts are stronger today in congressional elections than they were fifteen years ago.

7. The collective disadvantages of casework should not be exaggerated. True, district level staff has increased both absolutely and as a percentage of total *member* staff. However, if we include district staff as a percentage of total *congressional* staff, including committee staff and support agencies, differences disappear. Furthermore, constituency service is an important part of the representative relationship between member and constituent.

8. The one exception to this argument is the decline in the norm of seniority (which simply means that the most senior member of a committee gets to be the chair). Democrats violated this norm in the 1970s to remove several conservative southern Democrat chairs who were out of step with the party. Similarly, Newt Gingrich violated the seniority

norms for several key committee chairs in 1995 to make sure that he had loyalists rather than old-style, consensus-seeking Republicans at the helm. Thus, violating the norm of seniority can be an important tool for party leadership and collective decisionmaking.

9. The founders of Amway donated $1 million to the Republican National Party in the 1997–1998 cycle.

10. These respondents are clearly from the economic elite: almost half had annual incomes of more than $250,000, and over 80 percent had college degrees.

11. Normally, a bill must obtain approval from the committee of jurisdiction before it can come to the floor. Under a discharge petition, a simple majority (218 members) can force a bill to the floor over the committee's objection. When a bill comes to the floor under a discharge petition, the leadership lose their control over debate and amendments.

Chapter 4

1. Of course, pluralist theorists have been guilty of equating parts of Madisonian theory with their own. Most important is the divergent starting point: Madison was concerned with controlling the effects of "evil factions," while pluralists embraced factions as the essential embodiment of political action and expression of political interests.

2. Some of the material in this section was drawn from Canon, forthcoming.

3. However, Senator Roman Hruska of Nebraska challenged Griffith's argument. In defending President Nixon's appointee to the Supreme Court, G. Harrold Carswell, Hruska said, "Even if he were mediocre, there are a lot of mediocre judges and people and lawyers. They are entitled to a little representation, aren't they, and a little chance? We can't have all Brandeises and Frankfurters and Cardozos and stuff like that." (Barone, Ujifusa, and Matthews 1975, 494).

4. The technical term for this is the "motion to recommit with instructions."

5. These debates concern the economic impact of budget deficit through the "tax on capital" and interest rates, and the difference between budget deficits that are created to support long-term capital investment versus short-term spending such as transfer payments (such as Social Security or federal pensions).

Chapter 5

1. Data are from Ornstein, Mann, and Malbin (1998, table 3–10). Parties aided candidates in other ways, spending $65 million more on "coordinated expenditures" (defined as money spent on behalf of a candidate and in cooperation with the candidate's campaign), and "independent expenditures" (money spent on behalf of a candidate, but without any coordination with the candidate's campaign).

2. Currently, candidates can accept party money from national committees (the Republican National Committee and the Democratic National Committee), separate committees organized to help Senate and House candidates (the Democratic Congressional Campaign Committee, the Democratic Senate Campaign Committee, the Republican Congressional

Campaign Committee, and the Republican Senate Campaign Committee),and their state party organizations.

3. The survey of large campaign donors (over $200) that we described in Chapter 4 showed that this group is astonishingly unrepresentative of the general population: half of the large contributors had incomes nearly ten times that of the median household.

4. Some of the material in this section was drawn from Mayer (1995).

5. Madison went on to note that representatives may not always serve the public's interests, but this possibility, he argued, would be checked by the vast and extensive republic with its diverse interests (and the system of checks and balances and separation of powers).

6. This is precisely the argument made by supporters of Clinton's impeachment, who maintain that the House should not be deterred by the public's opposition to impeachment.

7. Similar levels of support were expressed for debates that were tied to specific pieces of legislation, with 44 percent strongly in favor and 26 percent opposed. One other interesting pattern was evident. About two-thirds of the forty-two freshmen who answered the survey were in favor of the debates, whereas only 21 percent and 23 percent of the members who had more than ten years' seniority were in favor of the "major issues" and specific legislation debates, respectively (U.S. Congress 1993, 272–273).

References

Adams, Greg D. 1996. Legislative Effects of Single-Member vs. Multi-Member Districts. *American Journal of Political Science* 40: 129–144.

Adams, Henry. 1946. *The Education of Henry Adams.* New York: Modern Library.

Aldrich, John H. 1995. *Why Parties? The Origin and Transformation of Party Politics in America.* Chicago: University of Chicago Press.

American Political Science Association (APSA). 1942. Congress—Problem, Diagnosis, Proposals: Second Progress Report of the American Political Science Association's Committee on Congress. *American Political Science Review* 36 (No. 6, December):1091–1102.

_____. 1945. *The Reorganization of Congress: A Report of the Committee on Congress of the American Political Science Association.* Washington, D.C.: Public Affairs Press.

Arnold, R. Douglas. 1990. *The Logic of Congressional Action.* New Haven: Yale University Press.

Axelrod, Robert M. 1984. *The Evolution of Cooperation.* New York: Basic Books.

Barkan, Joel D. 1995. Debate: PR and Southern Africa. Elections in Agrarian Societies. *Journal of Democracy* 6: 106–116.

Barone, Michael, and Grant Ujifusa. 1998. *The Almanac of American Politics 1998.* Washington, D.C.: National Journal.

Barone, Michael, Grant Ujifusa, and Douglas Matthews. 1975. *The Almanac of American Politics 1976.* New York: E. P. Dutton.

Bassett, John Spencer. 1922. James K. Polk and His Constituents, 1831–1832. *The American Historical Review* 28 (No.1, October): 68–77.

Bennett, James, and Allison Mitchell. 1998. "4 Who Said Yes on Impeaching Call for Censure." *New York Times.* December 22.

Benton's Abridgement of the Debates of Congress from 1789 to 1856. 1857. Vol. 2, 1796–1803. New York: D. Appleton & Co.

Berke, Richard L. 1998. Many Rising Stars Say Running for Congress Just Isn't Worth It. *New York Times* (March 15): 1.

Bessette, Joseph M. 1994. *The Mild Voice of Reason: Deliberative Democracy and American National Government.* Chicago: University of Chicago Press.

Bianco, William, David B. Spence, and John D. Wilkerson. 1996. The Electoral Connection in the Early Congress: The Case of the Compensation Act of 1816. *American Journal of Political Science* 40: 145–171.

Bickford, Charlene Bangs, Kenneth R. Bowling, and Helen E. Veit, eds. 1992. *Documentary History of the First Federal Congress.* Vol. X, *Debates in the House of Representatives: First Session, April-May 1789.* Baltimore: Johns Hopkins University Press.

Binder, Sarah A. 1995. Minority Rights. In *The Encyclopedia of the United States Congress.* Edited by Donald C. Bacon, Roger H. Davidson, and Morton Keller. New York: Simon and Schuster.

Binder, Sarah, A. 1996. The Partisan Basis of Procedural Choice: Allocating Parliamentary Rights in the House, 1789–1990. *American Political Science Review* 90: 8–20.

Binder, Sarah A., and Steven S. Smith. 1997. *Politics or Principle: Filibustering in the U.S. Senate.* Washington, D.C.: Brookings Institution.

Birnbaum, Jeffrey H., and Alan S. Murray. 1987. *Showdown at Gucci Gulch: Lawmakers, Lobbyists, and the Unlikely Triumph of Tax Reform.* New York: Vintage Books.

Blendon, Robert J., Mollyann Brodie, and John Benson. 1995. What Happened to Americans' Support for the Clinton Health Plan? *Health Affairs* 14 (No. 3, Summer): 7–23.

Blendon, Robert J., Mollyann Brodie, Tracy Stelzer Hyams, and John M. Benson. 1994. The American Public and the Critical Choices for Health System Reform. *The Journal of the American Medical Association* 271 (No. 19, May 18): 1539–1544.

Born, Richard. 1990. The Shared Fortunes of Congress and Congressmen: Members May Run, but They Can't Hide. *Journal of Politics* 52 (No. 4, November): 1223–1241.

Brinkley, Alan. 1997. The Challenge to Deliberative Democracy. In *The New Federalist Papers.* Edited by Alan Brinkley, Nelson W. Polsby, and Kathleen M. Sullivan. New York: W. W. Norton.

Bryce, James. 1921. *Modern Democracies.* Vol. 2. New York: MacMillan.

Bryd, Robert C. 1989. *The Senate, 1789–1989: Addresses on the History of the United States Senate.* Washington, D.C. Government Printing Office.

Burke, Edmund. 1774. "A Letter to John Farr and John Harris, Esqrs. Sheriffs of the City of Bristol on the Affairs of America." In *Edmund Burke: Selected Writings and Speeches.* Edited by Peter J. Stanlis. 1963 ed. New York: Doubleday Anchor.

Cain, Bruce E., John A. Ferejohn, and Morris P. Fiorina. 1984. The Constituency Basis of the Personal Vote for U.S. Representatives and British Members of Parliament. *American Political Science Review* 78 (No. 1, March):110–125.

———. 1987. *The Personal Vote: Constituency Service and Electoral Independence.* Cambridge, Mass.: Harvard University Press.

California Secretary of State. 1997. *1996 General Election: Campaign Finance for California State Candidates and Officeholders.* http://www.ss.ca.gov/prd/finance96/finance96.htm.

Canon, David T. Forthcoming. *Race, Redistricting, and Representation: The Unintended Consequences of Black Majority Districts in the U.S. House.* Chicago: University of Chicago Press.

Center for Responsive Politics. 1998. Tobacco Settlement Going Up in Smoke: Industry Vows to Snuff Out Deal in Congress, Where Its Money Speaks Loudly. (April 9).

Citizens' Research Foundation. 1996. *New Realities, New Thinking: Report of the Task Force on Campaign Finance Reform.* Los Angeles: Citizens' Research Foundation.

Cloud, David S. 1993. Big Risk for Margolies-Mezvinsky. *Congressional Quarterly Weekly Report* (August 7): 2125.

Collie, Melissa P., and Joseph Cooper. 1989. Multiple Referral and the "New" Committee System. In *Congress Reconsidered*. 4th ed. Edited by Lawrence C. Dodd and Bruce I. Oppenheimer. Washington, D.C.: CQ Press.

Cook, Timothy E. 1979. Legislature vs. Legislator: A Note on the Paradox of Congressional Support. *Legislative Studies Quarterly* 4: 43–52.

Corrado, Anthony, Thomas E. Mann, Daniel R. Ortiz, Trevor Potter, and Frank J. Sorauf. 1997. *Campaign Finance Reform: A Sourcebook*. Washington, D.C.: Brookings Institution.

Cox, Gary W., and Mathew D. McCubbins. 1993. *Legislative Leviathan: Party Government in the House*. Berkeley: University of California Press.

Crewe, Ivor. 1985. MPs and Their Constituents in Britain: How Strong the Links? In *Representatives of the People? Parliamentarians and Constituents in Western Democracies*. Edited by Vernon Bogdanor. London: Gower.

Cunningham, Noble E., Jr., ed. 1978. *Circular Letters of Congressmen to Their Constituents, 1789–1829*. 3 vols. Chapel Hill, N.C.: University of North Carolina Press.

Dahl, Robert A. 1956. *A Preface to Democratic Theory*. Chicago: University of Chicago Press.

Davidson, Chandler, and Bernard Grofman, eds. 1994. *Quiet Revolution in the South: The Impact of the Voting Rights Act, 1965–1990*. Princeton, N.J.: Princeton University Press.

de Toqueville, Alexis. 1945. *Democracy in America*. Vol I. New York: Alfred A. Knopf.

Denver, David, and Gordon Hands. 1997. *Modern Constituency Electioneering: Local Campaigning in the 1992 General Election*. London: Frank Cass.

Dodd, Lawrence C. 1986. The Cycle of Legislative Change: Building a Dynamic Theory. In *Political Science: The Science of Politics*. Edited by Herbert F. Weisberg. New York: Agathon.

————. 1993. Congress and the Politics of Renewal: Redressing the Crisis of Legitimation. In *Congress Reconsidered*. 5th ed. Edited by Lawrence C. Dodd and Bruce I. Oppenheimer. Washington, D.C.: Congressional Quarterly Press.

Donovan, Beth. 1994. Democrats' Overhaul Bill Dies on Senate Procedural Votes. *Congressional Quarterly Weekly Report* (October 1): 2757–2758.

Drew, Elizabeth. 1975. *Washington Journal: The Events of 1973–1974*. New York: Vintage.

Duncan, Philip D., and Christine C. Lawrence. 1995. *Politics in America 1996: The 104th Congress*. Washington, D.C.: Congressional Quarterly Press.

Ehrenhalt, Alan. 1991. *The United States of Ambition: Politicians, Power, and the Pursuit of Office*. New York: Times Books.

Elkins, Stanley, and Eric McKitrick. 1993. *The Age of Federalism: The Early American Republic, 1788–1800*. New York: Oxford University Press.

Evans, C. Lawrence, and Walter J. Oleszek. 1997. *Congress Under Fire: Reform Politics and the Republican Majority*. Boston: Houghton Mifflin.

Fallows, James. 1995. A Triumph of Misinformation. *Atlantic Monthly* (January): 26–37.

Federal Election Commission. 1996. *The FEC and the Federal Campaign Finance Law*. (August).

Fenno, Richard. 1973. *Congressmen in Committees.* Boston: Little, Brown.

Fenno, Richard. 1978. *Home Style: House Members in Their Districts.* Boston: Little, Brown.

Fenno, Richard F., Jr. 1975. If, as Ralph Nader Says, Congress Is "The Broken Branch," How Come We Love Our Congressmen So Much? In *Congress in Change.* Edited by Norman J. Ornstein. New York: Praeger.

Fiorina, Morris P. 1989. *Congress: Keystone of the Washington Establishment.* New Haven: Yale University Press.

Food and Drug Administration. 1995. *Background on Nicotine Pharmacology,* Appendix 1 to Proposed Rule Regarding FDA's Jurisdiction Over Nicotine-Containing Cigarettes and Smokeless Tobacco Products; Notice. *Federal Register* 60 (Friday August 11): 41314–41787.

Ford, Paul Leicester. 1899. *Writings of Thomas Jefferson, 1816–1826.* Vol X. New York: G. P. Putnam's Sons.

Forest, Benjamin. 1996. Where Should Democratic Compromise Take Place? *Social Science Quarterly* 77: 6–13.

Fudenberg, Drew, and Jean Tirole. 1991. *Game Theory.* Cambridge, Mass.: MIT Press.

Fuller, Bruce. 1909. *The Speakers of the House.* Boston: Little, Brown. Cited in William J. Keefe and Morris S. Ogul. 1997. *The American Legislative Process.* 9th ed. Upper Saddle River, N.J.: Prentice-Hall, 232.

Gamm, Gerald H., and Kenneth A. Shepsle. 1989. Emergence of Legislative Institutions: Standing Committees in the House and Senate, 1810–1825. *Legislative Studies Quarterly* 14: 39–66.

Gilmour, John B. 1992. Summits and Stalemates: Bipartisan Negotiations in the Post-reform Era. In *The Post-reform Congress.* Edited by Roger H. Davidson. New York: St. Martin's Press.

Gimpel, James G. 1996. *Fulfilling the Contract: The First 100 Days.* Needham Heights, Mass.: Allyn and Bacon.

Gingrich, Newt. 1988. Foreword. In *The Imperial Congress: Crisis in the Separation of Powers.* Edited by Gordon S. Jones and John A. Marini. New York: Pharos Books.

Ginsberg, Benjamin, and Martin Shefter. 1990. *Politics by Other Means.* New York: Basic Books.

Grann, David. 1998. Broken Rules. *New Republic* (April 6): 12–14.

Green, John, Paul Herrnson, Lynda Powell, and Clyde Wilcox. 1998. *Individual Congressional Campaign Contributors: Wealthy, Conservative—and Reform-Minded.* Chicago: Joyce Foundation.

Greenblatt, Alan. 1998. Growing Ranks of Cigarette Tax Critics Invigorate Big Tobacco's Lobbying Effort. *Congressional Quarterly Weekly Report* (May 16): 1306–1308.

Guinier, Lani. 1994. *The Tyranny of the Majority: Fundamental Fairness in Representative Democracy.* New York: Free Press.

Hall, Richard L. 1996. *Participation in Congress.* New Haven: Yale University Press.

Hamilton, Alexander, James Madison, and John Jay. 1961. *The Federalist Papers.* New American Library ed. New York: Times Mirror.

Hammond, Michael E., and Peter M. Wyerich. 1988. "Legislative Lords: Gag Rules and Permanent Staff." In *The Imperial Congress: Crisis in the Separation of Powers*. Edited by Gordon S. Jones and John A. Marini. New York: Pharos Books.

Harlow, Ralph Volney. 1917. *The History of Legislative Methods in the Period Before 1825*. New Haven: Yale University Press.

Harris, Fred. 1995. *In Defense of Congress*. New York: St. Martin's Press.

Hess, Stephen. 1994. The Decline and Fall of Congressional News. In *Congress, the Press, and the Public*. Edited by Thomas E. Mann and Norman J. Ornstein. Washington, D.C.: American Enterprise Institute and the Brookings Institution.

Heymann, Phillip, and Jody Heymann. 1996. The Fate of Public Debate in the United States. *Harvard Journal on Legislation* 33 (No. 2, Summer): 516–517.

Hibbing, John R, and Elizabeth Thiess-Morse. 1995. *Congress as Public Enemy: Public Attitudes Toward American Political Institutions*. New York: Cambridge University Press.

Himmelfarb, Richard. 1995. *Catastrophic Politics: The Rise and Fall of the Medicare Catastrophic Coverage Act of 1988*. University Park, Pa.: Pennsylvania State University Press.

Horowitz, Donald. 1991. *A Democratic South Africa? Constitutional Engineering in a Divided Society*. Berkeley: University of California Press.

House of Representatives. 1994. Voting Rights Roundtable, House Subcommittee on Civil and Consitutional Rights, Committee on the Judiciary. Washington, D.C.: mimeo (May 25).

Issacharoff, Samuel, and Richard H. Pildes. 1996. All for One: Can Cumulative Voting Ease Racial Tensions? *The New Republic* (November 18): 10.

Jacobs, Lawrence R., and Robert Y. Shapiro. 1994. Questioning the Conventional Wisdom on Public Opinion Toward Health Reform. *PS: Political Science and Politics* 27 (No. 2, January): 208–214.

Jacobs, Lawrence R., Eric D. Lawrence, Robert Shapiro, and Steven S. Smith. 1995. Congressional Perceptions of Public Opinion and Health Reform. Paper presented at the 1995 annual meeting of the American Political Science Association, August 31–September 3, Chicago, Illinois.

Jewell, Malcolm E. 1983. Legislator-Constituent Relations and the Representative Process. *Legislative Studies Quarterly* 13: 303–337.

Jones, Charles O. 1994. *The President in a Separated System*. Washington, D.C.: Brookings Institution.

_____. 1995. Cannon Revolt. In *The Encylopedia of the United States Congress*. Edited by Donald C. Bacon, Roger H. Davidson, and Morton Keller. New York: Simon and Schuster.

Kaplan, Dave, and Julianna Gruenwald. 1994. Longtime "Second Party" Scores a Long List of GOP Firsts. *Congressional Quarterly Weekly Report* (November 12): 3232–3239.

Katz, Jeffrey L. 1998. Petition Pushes House GOP Leadership to Schedule Campaign Finance Debate. *Congressional Quarterly Weekly Report* (April 25): 1057–1058.

Keefe, William J., and Morris K. Ogul. 1997. *The American Legislative Process: Congress and the States*. Upper Saddle River, N.J.: Prentice Hall, 9th edition.

Kenyon, Cecilia M. 1955. Men of Little Faith: The Anti-Federalists on the Nature of Representative Government. *William and Mary Quarterly* 12 (No. 1, January): 3–43.

Kettl, Donald F. 1986. *Leadership at the Fed.* New Haven: Yale University Press.

King, David C. 1997. *Turf Wars: How Congressional Committees Claim Jurisdiction.* Chicago: University of Chicago Press.

Kirby, James C., Jr. 1970. *Congress and the Public Trust.* Report of the Association of the Bar of the City of New York Special Committee on Congressional Ethics. New York: Atheneum Press.

Koszczuk, Jackie. 1997. Coup Attempt Throws GOP Off Legislative Track. *Congressional Quarterly Weekly Report* (July 19): 1671–1674.

Krehbiel, Keith. 1991. *Information and Legislative Organization.* Ann Arbor: University of Michigan Press.

Lardeyret, Guy. 1991. The Problem with PR. *Journal of Democracy* 2: 30–35.

Laundy, Phillip. 1997. *Parliament and the People: The Reality and the Public Perception.* Aldershot, England: Ashgate.

Leigh, David, and Ed Vullamy. 1997. *Sleaze: The Corruption of Parliament.* London: Fourth Estate.

Letter to the Electors of England on the Necessity of Reform in the Representation of the People, Containing Some Expedients Calculated to Produce It. 1809. London: J. Budd.

Levin, Myron, and Henry Weinstein. 1998. Last of 46 State Officials Sign Tobacco Accord. *Los Angeles Times.* November 21.

Lieberman, Joseph. 1998. A Republic—If We Can Keep It. *Atlantic Monthly* (July): 14–17.

Lijphart, Arend. 1998. Reforming the House: Three Moderately Radical Proposals. *PS: Political Science and Politics* 30: 10–13.

Lippmann, Walter. 1922. *Public Opinion.* New York: Free Press.

Loomis, Burdett. 1998. *The Contemporary Congress.* 2d ed. New York: St. Martin's Press.

Loomis, Burdett. 1988. *The New American Politician: Ambition, Entrepreneurship, and the Changing Face of Political Life.* New York: Basic Books.

Los Angeles Times. 1998. Term Limits' Downside. September 18. Editorial.

Luce, Robert. 1926. *Congress: An Explanation.* Cambridge, Mass.: Harvard University Press.

Luneberg, William V., ed. 1998. *The Lobbying Manual: A Compliance Guide for Lawyers and Lobbyists.* 2d ed. Chicago: American Bar Association, Section of Administrative Law and Regulatory Practice.

MacNeil, Neil. 1963. *Forge of Democracy: The House of Representatives.* New York: David McKay Company, Inc.

Mann, Thomas E., and Norman J. Ornstein. 1992. *Renewing Congress: A First Report.* Washington D.C.: American Enterprise Institute.

———. 1993. *Renewing Congress: A Second Report.* Washington D.C.: American Enterprise Institute.

Matland, Richard E., and Donley T. Studlar. 1996. The Contagion of Women Candidates in Single-Member District and Proportional Representation Electoral Systems: Canada and Norway. *Journal of Politics* 58: 707–733.

Mayer, Kenneth R. 1995. Closing Military Bases (Finally): Solving Collective Dilemmas Through Delegation. *Legislative Studies Quarterly* 20 (No. 3, August 1995): 393–413.

Mayhew, David R. 1974. *Congress: The Electoral Connection.* New Haven: Yale University Press.

McBride, Ann. 1998. Statement of Common Cause President Ann McBride on How Campaign Money Drives the Tobacco Debate. Common Cause Press Release. June 15.

Mill, John Stuart. 1910. *Utilitarianism, Liberty, and Representative Government.* Everyman's Library ed. London: J. M. Dent & Sons, Ltd.

Monroe, Kristin Renwick. 1991. The Theory of Rational Action. In *The Economic Approach to Politics.* Edited by Kristin Renwick Monroe. New York: Harper Collins.

Morrill, Richard L. 1996. Territory, Community, and Collective Representation. *Social Science Quarterly* 77: 3–5.

Nation. 1897. January 28.

Neikirk, William. 1998. G.O.P. Wooing Main St., Not Wall St., *Chicago Tribune* (June 15): 1.

O'Dwyer, Margaret M. 1964. A French Diplomat's View of Congress, 1790. *William and Mary Quarterly.* 3d series. 21 (No. 3, July): 408–444.

Ohline, Howard A. 1980. Slavery, Economics, and Congressional Politics, 1790. *Journal of Southern History* XLVI: 335–360. Reprinted in Joel Sibley, ed. 1991. *The Congress of the United States: Its Origins and Early Development.* Brooklyn N.Y.: Carlson Publishing.

Oliver, Dawn. 1997. Regulating the Conduct of MPs. The British Experience of Combating Corruption. In *Political Corruption.* Edited by Paul Heywood. Oxford, England: Blackwell Publishers.

Olson, Allison G. 1992. Eighteenth Century Colonial Legislatures and Their Constituents. *The Journal of American History* 79 (No. 2, September): 543–567.

_____. 1983. The Virginia Merchants of London: A Study in Eighteenth-Century Interest-Group Politics. *William and Mary Quarterly.* 3d series. 40 (No. 3, July): 363–388.

Ornstein, Norman J. 1998. The Beauty of Closed Doors. *New York Times.* (October 9): 27.

Ornstein, Norman J., Thomas E. Mann, and Michael J. Malbin. 1998. *Vital Statistics on Congress 1997–1998.* Washington, D.C.: Congressional Quarterly Press.

Ostrom, Eleanor. 1990. *Governing the Commons: The Evolution of Institutions for Collective Action.* New York: Cambridge University Press.

Palazzolo, Daniel. 1995. House Leadership. In *The Encyclopedia of the United States Congress.* 4 vols. Edited by Donald C. Bacon, Roger H. Davidson, and Morton Keller. New York: Simon and Schuster.

Parker, Glenn R. 1981. Can Congress Ever Be a Popular Institution? In *The House at Work.* Edited by Joseph Cooper and G. Calvin Mackenzie. Austin: University of Texas Press.

Parker, Glenn R., and Roger H. Davidson. 1979. Why Do Americans Love Their Congressmen So Much More Than Their Congress? *Legislative Studies Quarterly* 4: 53–61.

Penny, Timothy J., and Major Garrett. 1995. *Common Cents: A Retiring Six-Term Congressman Reveals How Congress Really Works—and What We Must Do to Fix It.* Boston: Little, Brown and Co.

Perkins, John A. 1944. American Government and Politics: Congressional Self-Improvement. *American Political Science Review* 38: 499–511.

Peters, Ronald M., Jr. 1997. *The American Speakership: The Office in Historical Perspective.* 2d ed. Baltimore: Johns Hopkins University Press.

Peterson, Mark. 1995. The Health Care Debate: All Heat and No Light. *Journal of Health, Politics, Policy & Law* 20 (No. 2, Summer): 424–425.

Phillips, Anne. 1995. *The Politics of Presence.* New York: Clarendon Press/Oxford University Press.

Polsby, Nelson W. 1968. The Institutionalization of the U.S. House of Representatives. *American Political Science Review* 62 (No. 1, March): 144–168.

Rae, Nicol C. 1998. *Conservative Reformers: The Republican Freshmen and the Lessons of the 104th Congress.* Armonk, N.Y.: M.E. Sharpe.

Rakove, Jack. 1987. The Structure of Politics at the Accession of George Washington. In *Beyond Confederation: Origins of the Constitution and American National Identity.* Edited by Richard Beeman et al. Chapel Hill: University of North Carolina Press. Reprinted in Joel Sibley, ed. 1991. *The Congress of the United States: Its Origins and Early Development.* Brooklyn, N.Y.: Carlson Publishing.

_____. 1996. *Original Meanings: Politics and Ideas in the Making of the Constitution.* New York: Alfred A. Knopf.

Rauch, Jonathan. 1994. *Demosclerosis: The Silent Killer of American Government.* New York: Times Books.

Rieselbach, Leroy N. 1977. *Congressional Reform in the Seventies.* Morristown, N.J.: General Learning Press.

_____. 1994. *Congressional Reform: The Changing Modern Congress.* Washington, D.C.: CQ Press.

Rohde, David W. 1991. *Parties and Leaders in the Postreform House.* Chicago: University of Chicago Press.

Rothenberg, Stuart. 1998. Will November Bring Big Incumbent Wave or Small Partisan Currents? *Roll Call Monthly* (June): 1.

Rubin, Allisa J. 1994. Mixed Signals. *Congressional Quarterly Weekly Report* (July 9): 1871.

_____. 1994. Overhaul Issue Unlikely to Rest in Peace. *Congressional Quarterly Weekly Report* (October 1): 2797–2801.

Rule, Wilma. 1994. Women's Underrepresentation and Electoral Systems. *PS: Political Science & Politics* 27: 689–692.

Rule, Wilma, and Joseph F. Zimmerman, eds. 1994. *Electoral Systems in Comparative Perspective: Their Impact on Women and Minorities.* Westport, Conn.: Greenwood Press.

Safire, William. 1976. *Safire's Political Dictionary.* New York: Ballantine Books.

Sandler, Todd. 1992. *Collective Action: Theory and Applications.* Ann Arbor: University of Michigan Press.

Sawyer, Jack, and Duncan MacRae Jr. 1962. Game Theory and Cumulative Voting in Illinois: 1902–1954. *American Political Science Review* 56: 936–946.

Schneider, William. 1989. JFK's Children: The Class of '74. *Atlantic Monthly* (March): 35–58.

Schoenbrod, David. 1993. *Power Without Responsibility: How Congress Abuses the People Through Delegation*. New Haven: Yale University Press.

Schram, Martin. 1995. *Speaking Freely: Former Members of Congress Talk About Money in Politics*. Washington, D.C.: Center for Responsive Politics.

Schuman, Howard E. 1992. *Politics and the Budget: The Struggle Between the President and the Congress*. Englewood Cliffs, N.J.: Prentice-Hall.

Schwartz, John. 1998. Jury Imposes Damages on Tobacco Firm. *Washington Post* (June 10): A1.

Senate Hearing 103–26. 1993. Hearing Before the Joint Committee on the Organization of Congress. Operations of the Congress: Testimony of Hon. Robert C. Byrd, Hon. Christopher S. Bond, Hon. Charles E. Grassley, and Hon. Hank Brown. 103rd Cong., 1st sess.

Senate Hearing 103–128. 1993. Hearing before the Joint Committee on the Organization of Congress. Open Days for Members and Outside Groups. 103rd Cong., 1st sess.

Senate Report 1414. 1966. Joint Committee on the Organization of the Congress, Final Report. 89th Cong., 2nd sess.

Sharp, James Roger. 1993. *American Politics in the Early Republic*. New Haven: Yale University Press.

Shastri, Amita. 1991. Electoral Competition and Minority Alienation in a Plurality System: Sri Lanka 1947–77. *Electoral Studies* 10: 326–347.

Shugart, Matthew, and John Carey. 1992. *Presidents and Assemblies: Constitutional Design and Electoral Dynamics*. New York: Cambridge University Press.

Skeen, C. Edward. 1986. *Vox Populi, Vox Dei*: The Compensation Act of 1816 and the Rise of Popular Politics. *Journal of the Early Republic* 6 (Fall): 387–408.

Skocpol, Theda. 1996. *Boomerang: Clinton's Health Security Effort and the Turn Against Government in U.S. Politics*. New York: W. W. Norton & Company.

Smith, James Morton. 1956. *Freedom's Fetters: The Alien and Sedition Laws and American Civil Liberties*. Ithaca, N.Y.: Cornell University Press.

Smith, Robert C. 1990. Recent Elections and Black Politics: The Maturation or Death of Black Politics? *PS: Political Science and Politics* 23: 160–162.

Smith, Steven S. 1989. *Call to Order: Floor Politics in the House and Senate*. Washington, D.C.: Brookings Institution.

Steinmo, Sven, and Jon Watts. 1995. It's the Institutions, Stupid! Why Comprehensive National Health Insurance Always Fails in America. *Journal of Health Politics, Policy, and Law* 20 (No. 2, Summer): 329–372.

Sullivan, Kathleen M. 1997. What's Wrong with Constitutional Amendments? In *The New Federalist Papers*. Edited by Alan Brikley, Nelson W. Polsby, and Kathleen M. Sullivan..

Swift, Elaine K. 1996. *The Making of an American Senate*. Ann Arbor: University of Michigan Press.

Tacheron, Donald G., and Morris K. Udall. 1966. *The Job of Congressman: An Introduction to Service in the U.S. House of Representatives*. Indianapolis, Ind.: Bobbs-Merrill.

Thernstrom, Abigail. 1987. *Whose Votes Count? Affirmative Action and Minority Voting Rights.* Cambridge, Mass.: Harvard University Press.

Thomas, Rosarita Maria. 1992. Public Attitudes Toward Congress: Why the Decline? In *Congressional Reorganization: Options for Change.* Washington, D.C.:Congressional Research Service (Report prepared for the Joint Committee on the Organization of Congress).

Thomas, Sue, and Clyde Wilcox, eds. 1998. *Women and Elective Office: Past, Present, and Future.* New York: Oxford University Press.

Thompson, Dennis F. 1995. *Ethics in Congress: From Individual to Institutional Corruption.* Washington, D.C.: Brookings Institution.

Torry, Saundra. 1998. Fearing Gain for Trial Lawyers, Business Groups Fight Tobacco Bill Harder. *Washington Post* (May 19): A5.

U.S. Congress. 1986. House Committee on Energy and Commerce. *Petitions, Memorials, and Other Documents Submitted for the Consideration of Congress, March 4, 1789 to December 14, 1795.* Committee Print 99-AA. 99th Cong., 2nd sess.

U.S. Congress. 1993. Joint Committee on the Organization of Congress. *Organization of the Congress.* H. Rept. 103–413. 103d Cong., 1st sess. December.

U.S. Congress. 1997. House Committee on Standards of Official Conduct. *Summary of Activities: One Hundred Fourth Congress.* H. Rept. 104–886. 104th Cong., 2nd sess.

U.S. Department of Defense. 1998. *The Report of the Department of Defense on Base Realignment and Closure.* Washington, D.C.: Government Printing Office. April.

Uslaner, Eric M. 1993. *The Decline of Comity in Congress.* Ann Arbor: University of Michigan Press.

Van Biema, David. 1994. One Person, Seven Votes. *Time* 143 (No. 17, April 25): 42–43.

Wattenberg, Martin P. 1996. *The Decline of American Political Parties: 1952–1994.* Cambridge, Mass.: Harvard University Press.

_____. 1992. *The Rise of Candidate-Centered Politics: Presidential Elections of the 1980s.* Cambridge, Mass.: Harvard University Press.

Weaver, Leon. 1986. The Rise, Decline, and Resurrection of Proportional Representation in Local Government in the United States. In *Electoral Laws and Their Political Consequences.* Edited by Bernard Grofman and Arend Lijphart. New York: Agathon Press, 139–153.

West, Darrell M. 1997. *Air Wars: Television Advertising in Election Campaigns: 1953–1996.* Washington, D.C.: CQ Press.

Wharton, Francis. 1849. *State Trials of the United States During the Administrations of Washington and Adams.* Philadelphia: Carey and Hart.

White, Joseph. 1995. Commentary: The Horse and the Jumps: Comments on the Health Care Reform Steeplechase. *Journal of Health Politics, Policy, and Law* 20 (No. 2, Summer): 373–383.

Wiley, Alexander. 1947. *Laughing with Congress.* New York: Crown Publishers.

Wood, Gordon S. 1969. *The Creation of the American Republic, 1776–1787.* Chapel Hill, N.C.: University of North Carolina Press.

Yankelovich, Daniel. 1995. The Debate That Wasn't: The Public and the Clinton Plan. *Health Affairs* 14 (No. 1, Spring): 7–23.

Young, James Sterling. 1966. *The Washington Community, 1800–1828.* New York: Columbia University Press.

Zimmerman, Joseph F., and Wilma Rule. 1998. A More Representative United States House of Representatives? *PS: Political Science and Politics* 30: 5–10.

Index